CHILDREN'S
QUICK
& EASY
COOK
BOOK

BY
ANGELA WILKES

DK

DORLING KINDERSLEY
LONDON • NEW YORK • MOSCOW • SYDNEY

A DORLING KINDERSLEY BOOK

EDITORS
Rachel Harrison, Mary Atkinson

ART EDITORS
Mary Sandberg, Claire Penny

ADDITIONAL DESIGN
Michelle Baxter, Susan Calver,
Karen Chapman, Helen Melville

DEPUTY MANAGING ART EDITOR
Jane Horne

SENIOR MANAGING EDITOR
Sheila Hanly

PHOTOGRAPHY
Amanda Haywood, Clive Streeter,
Norman Hollands, Dave King

HOME ECONOMISTS
Nicola Fowler, Emma Jane Frost,
Emma Patmore

PRODUCTION
Josie Alabaster

DTP DESIGNERS
Almudena Díaz, Nicola Studdart

4 6 8 10 9 7 5

First published in Great Britain in 1997
by Dorling Kindersley Limited,
9 Henrietta Street, London WC2E 8PS

Copyright © 1997 Dorling Kindersley Limited, London
Text copyright © 1997 Angela Wilkes
Visit us on the World Wide Web at http://www.dk.com

A CIP catalogue record for this book
is available from the British Library.

ISBN: 0-7513-5651-4

Colour reproduction by Bright Arts, Hong Kong
Printed and bound in Italy by Graphicom

Dorling Kindersley would like to thank:
Emma Price-Thomas, Rachel Wardley, and Sarah Phillips
for additional editorial help; Amanda Harrold, Nicola
Harrold, Stacey Martin, Sarah Mendham, Natasha Payne,
Sam Priddy, and David Watts for modelling.

CONTENTS

SUPER-FAST SNACKS

BAGEL BONANZA　　　12
These traditional Jewish bread rolls
can have sweet or savoury fillings
and make an ideal breakfast or snack.

CROISSANT FEAST　　　13
Delicious, buttery French croissants
filled with either cream and jam,
chocolate, or ham and cheese.

CRUNCHY CROSTINI　　　14
Tiny pieces of Italian-style toasted
bread with lots of tasty savoury
toppings to choose from.

TRIPLE-DECKER DOORSTOPPERS   15

Three delicious sandwiches piled high enough to satisfy any hunger.

PITTA POCKETS   18

Three scrumptious filling ideas for these Middle-Eastern flat breads, which open out like pockets.

COOL CATS   21

These tasty fillets of fish tucked into slices of French bread make a fun alternative to hot dogs.

POPCORN TREATS   16

How to pop your own corn and use it to make cheesy popcorn and maple peanut popcorn.

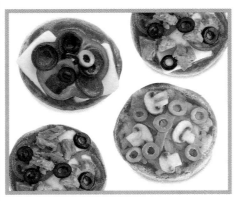

CHEATS' PIZZAS   19

Create your own tiny pizzas using muffins and choosing from the wide variety of suggested toppings.

FRUIT SMOOTHIES AND ICE-CREAM SODA   22-23

Two ideas for long, cool drinks to sip on hot summer days.

CHUNKY CHIPS   17

A quick, safe, and healthy way to make delicious chips by roasting them in the oven.

HOT DOGS WITH SALSA   20

This classic fast-food snack is even more delicious when made at home and served with spicy tomato salsa.

SUNSHINE TOAST   24

Brighten up your mornings with this clever alternative to the traditional breakfast egg.

SPEEDY MEALS

CLASSIC OMELETTES 26-27
Two very different omelettes: a quick cheese omelette and a tasty Spanish omelette, called a tortilla.

PERFECT PASTA 32-33
Pasta and sliced sausages baked in a delicious tomato sauce make this a hearty evening meal.

FISHCAKE FLOUNDERS 36-37
Tasty tuna and potato fishcakes, cooked with a crunchy crust made from fresh breadcrumbs.

VEGETABLE SOUPS 28-29
Two tasty vegetable soups: a summery pea soup and a thick carrot and orange soup.

TURKISH MEATBALLS 34
Spicy Middle-Eastern meatballs made from minced lamb and grilled on skewers.

CHICKEN NUGGETS 38
Bite-sized nuggets of tender chicken coated in fresh breadcrumbs and shallow-fried.

TACOS AND GUACAMOLE 30-31
Crisp Mexican pancakes with two spicy fillings and an avocado dip.

FALAFEL 35
Spicy chick-pea fritters packed into pitta bread and served with minted yogurt, cucumber, and tomato.

LEMONY FISH FINGERS 39
A crisp lemon-and-herb coating makes these fresh fish fingers a tasty change to shop-bought varieties.

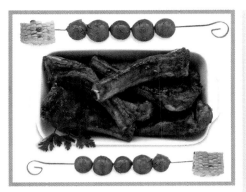

BARBECUED BITES   40-41
Marinated spare ribs, tomato kebabs, and seasoned sweetcorn to cook on a barbecue or under a grill.

THAI KEBABS WITH SATAY SAUCE   46-47
Thai-style pork, chicken, and prawn kebabs with a peanut butter sauce.

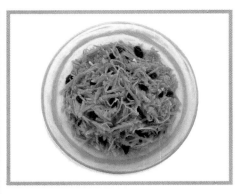

CARROT SALAD   51
A really crunchy salad made with grated carrots, lots of raisins, and toasted sunflower seeds.

CHICKEN CHOW-MEIN   42-43
Chinese noodles stir-fried with sliced chicken and lots of vegetables.

SALADE NIÇOISE   48-49
This salad from the south of France, made with tuna, potatoes, tomatoes, and olives, is a light meal in itself.

SAVOURY PANCAKES   52-53
A basic light pancake recipe and two ideas for savoury fillings: cheese and ham or creamy mushroom.

CHICKEN CURRY AND RICE   44-45
A mild and creamy chicken curry served with spicy rice.

TABBOULEH   50
This exotic salad from north Africa is made with bulgur wheat, cucumber, mint, and parsley.

SPICY CHICKEN BURGERS 54
Fried spicy chicken served in a sesame-seed bun with lettuce, soured cream, and tomato relish.

PERFECT PUDDINGS

PROFITEROLES 56-57
A pile of light, easy-to-make buns filled with whipped cream and smothered in chocolate sauce.

LEMON CHEESECAKE 60-61
A wonderfully light, lemon-flavoured cheesecake baked in the oven, then chilled in the fridge.

FRUIT CRUMBLE 64
This traditional baked dessert has a juicy apple-and-blackberry filling and a crunchy topping.

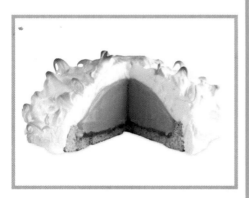

BAKED ALASKA 58
A magical mound of ice cream, sponge, and snowy peaks of meringue, baked in the oven.

TIRAMISU 62
A rich Italian pudding made with cream cheese, sponge, coffee, and grated chocolate.

FRUIT SALAD 65
Fresh pineapple, melon, grapes, and mango give this fruit salad an exciting tropical flavour.

KNICKERBOCKER GLORIES 59
Tall, cool ice-cream sundaes: strawberry or banoffee flavour.

CLAFOUTI 63
This traditional French pudding is made with fresh plums baked in a bed of sponge.

HOT CHOCOLATE PUDS 66
An easy recipe for making four little chocolate soufflés that look incredibly impressive.

TREATS AND SWEETS

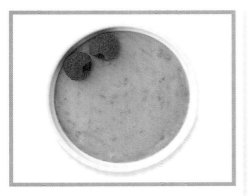

RASPBERRY FOOLS 67
A delicious and very quick summer dessert made of crushed raspberries and whipped cream.

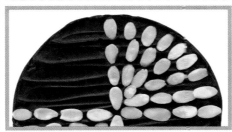

ULTIMATE CHOCOLATE CAKE 72-73
A rich, gooey chocolate and almond cake that would impress a top chef.

FLAPJACKS 78-79
Three varieties of this popular crunchy oat bar: plain, fruit and nut, and chocolate.

TOTALLY TERRIFIC TRIFLE 68-69
A favourite English dessert made with sponge, fruit, custard, and cream.

FROSTED CARROT CAKE 74-75
A delicious, moist cake with cream cheese frosting and fun decorations.

STAINED-GLASS COOKIES 80
These amazing shortbread cookies with "stained-glass" centres look festive and taste good, too.

FRUITY CRÈME BRÛLÉES 70
Fresh fruit topped with creamy yogurt and a crisp caramel crust.

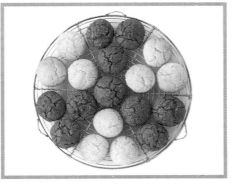

MACAROONS 76-77
These little almond biscuits melt in the mouth. Choose between plain macaroons or the chocolate variety.

CHOCOLATE DIPS 81
Fresh orange zest gives these simple yet elegant biscuits a subtle zing that goes well with the chocolate tip.

RASPBERRY MUFFINS   82
Delicious, puffy, American-style muffins studded with raspberries and nuggets of white chocolate.

FLORENTINES   86
Exotic biscuits made from chopped fruit and nuts set in toffee and coated with chocolate.

FRUIT AND NUT BALLS   89
Apricots, raisins, almonds, coconut, and white chocolate flavour these tasty little sweets.

PECAN PUFFS   83
Irresistible, light-as-a-feather cookies made from pecan nuts and dusted with icing sugar.

CHOCOLATE CRISPY CAKES   87
Really easy cakes to make, using just breakfast cereal and chocolate.

PEANUT BUTTER SWEETS   90
Fudgy, peanut butter-flavoured sweets coated in chocolate.

TASTY TARTS   84-85
Two types of tart: simple jam tarts and more sophisticated fresh fruit and cream tarts.

CHOCOLATE TRUFFLES   88
A quick and easy version of these famous chocolate sweets with three delicious coatings.

PEPPERMINT CREAMS   91
Easy-to-make, peppermint-flavoured sweets in pretty pastel colours or dipped in chocolate.

BEFORE YOU START

The CHILDREN'S QUICK AND EASY COOKBOOK is packed full of delicious, easy-to-follow recipes that anyone can make. From tasty snacks to scrumptious puddings, there is something for every occasion.

HOW TO USE THIS BOOK

You will find a quick description of all the recipes in the book on pages 2 to 8. Every recipe lists the equipment and ingredients you need, and shows you step-by-step exactly what to do. All the main cooking terms are shown in italic type, like this: *simmer*. You can look up the meaning of these cooking terms in the step-by-step picture glossary on pages 92 to 95.

WEIGHING AND MEASURING

Every recipe gives both metric and imperial measurements. Keep to one set of measurements throughout a recipe, as it is not possible to convert one set of measurements to the other exactly. A "spoonful" in this book means a level spoonful.

USING THE COOKER

Always ask an adult to turn on the oven for you. Sometimes the oven needs to be switched on to the temperature given in the recipe before you start cooking, so it has time to heat up. Temperatures for electric ovens are shown in Celsius (°C) and Fahrenheit (°F). For gas ovens the temperature is shown in gas marks. Always follow the cooking time given in the recipe, and don't forget to turn off the oven at the end.

BE CAREFUL!

Never cook anything unless there is an adult to help you. This oven glove symbol is a safety warning. Whenever you see it next to a picture, ask an adult for help and remember to be extra careful.

KEY TO SYMBOLS

At the top of each recipe you will see some of the following symbols. They give you quick information about the recipe.

This symbol shows you how long it will take to prepare the recipe.

This symbol shows you how long it will take to grill or bake the food.

This symbol shows you how many people the recipe serves, or what quantity it makes.

This symbol shows you the oven temperature you should use.

KITCHEN RULES

1 Before you start cooking, wash your hands and put on an apron. You may need to roll up your sleeves as well.

2 Collect all the ingredients together. Weigh the dry ingredients and measure liquids in a measuring jug.

3 Be very careful with sharp knives. Hold them with the blade pointing downwards and always use a chopping board.

4 When you are cooking on top of the cooker, turn the saucepan handles to the side so that you do not knock them.

5 When you are stirring food in a saucepan, use a wooden spoon and hold the saucepan firmly by the handle.

6 Always wear oven gloves when picking up anything hot, or when putting things into or taking them out of the oven.

7 Have a space ready for hot things. Put them on a mat or a wooden board, not straight on to a table or work surface.

8 Always make sure your hands are dry before you plug in or disconnect an electric gadget, such as a blender.

9 Wash up as you go along, and wipe up any spills straight away. Each time you handle a different food, wash your hands afterwards.

SUPER-FAST
SNACKS

BAGEL BONANZA

You will need

Chopping board • Bread knife
Grill pan • Knife • Spoon

Ingredients

 1 or 2 bagels per person

Suggested fillings

Cream cheese

Sliced salami

Cherry compote

Sliced banana

Grated Cheddar cheese

Sliced tomato

What to do

1 Cut the bagels in half. Heat the grill and toast the bagels lightly, cut sides up, until the edges are golden brown.

2 Layer the bases with the filling of your choice, then put the lids on the bagels and eat them while they're still warm.

To make this bagel, fill it with cream cheese and sliced salami.

The base of this bagel was covered in grated cheese, topped with tomato and then grilled.

This bagel was filled with cherry compote and sliced banana.

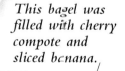

CROISSANT FEAST

You will need

Grill pan • Chopping board
Bread knife • Knife • Grater

Ingredients

 1 or 2 croissants
per person

Suggested fillings

 Crème fraîche

Strawberry jam

Dark chocolate

Sliced ham

Grated Cheddar cheese

Tasty tips

Try different sorts of jam in the jam croissant, or use stewed apple or fruit compote instead. In the cheese croissant, try other cheeses, such as Gruyère.

What to do

Warm the croissants in the oven or under the grill, then cut them in half and spread with the filling of your choice.

This croissant was made by spreading the base with a layer of crème fraîche and topping it with strawberry jam.

To make this delicious croissant, sprinkle grated dark chocolate on the base, warm it under the grill for a minute and then add the lid.

Make this savoury croissant by laying a slice of ham on the base, sprinkling grated cheese on top, and grilling it for a minute before adding the lid.

CRUNCHY CROSTINI

You will need

Chopping board • Bread knife
Grill pan • Sharp knife
Small bowl • Pastry brush

Ingredients

1 baguette/
French bread stick

1 clove garlic

Olive oil

Suggested toppings

Tomato passata or sauce

Sliced mozzarella cheese

Sliced tomatoes

Hummus

Sliced pitted black olives

Parsley

Green pesto

Sliced cherry tomatoes

Tinned tuna fish

Chopped celery

Chives

Sliced mozzarella cheese

Sliced ham

Soft cream or
curd cheese

Sliced salami

What to do

1 Heat the grill. Carefully cut the baguette into slices, then toast the pieces of bread on both sides until golden brown.

2 Rub one side of each piece of toast with half a clove of garlic, brush it with olive oil, and add the topping of your choice.

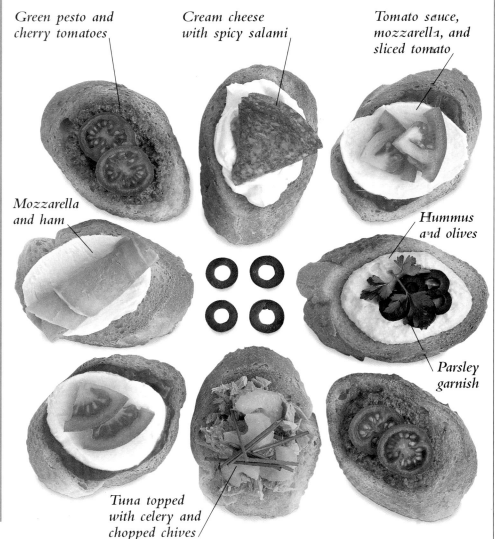

Green pesto and cherry tomatoes

Cream cheese with spicy salami

Tomato sauce, mozzarella, and sliced tomato

Mozzarella and ham

Hummus and olives

Parsley garnish

Tuna topped with celery and chopped chives

TRIPLE-DECKER DOORSTOPPERS

You will need

Chopping board • Knife
Spoon • Bread knife

Spicy doorstopper

3 slices bread

Butter

Sliced cold chicken

Diced cucumber and chopped mint in natural yogurt

Mango chutney

Festive doorstopper

3 slices bread
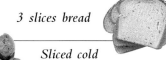

Sliced cold cooked sausage

Mayonnaise

Sliced cold turkey

Cranberry sauce

Tricolour doorstopper

3 slices bread

Sliced mozzarella cheese

Sliced tomato

Sliced avocado

French dressing

What to do

1 If your sandwich has butter or mayonnaise in it, spread it over the bread. Layer half the ingredients over one slice.

2 Add the second slice of bread, then another layer of ingredients. Add the third slice, then cut the sandwich in quarters.

Brown bread was used to make this spicy doorstopper.

To make this festive doorstopper, spread the bread with mayonnaise. Lettuce can be added for extra colour.

A cocktail stick helps hold the sandwich together.

The tricolour doorstopper gets its name from its three bright colours: red, white, and green.

POPCORN TREATS

You will need

Large saucepan with lid
Small saucepan • Wooden spoon

Ingredients

2 tablespoons
vegetable oil

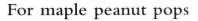

55 g (2 oz)
popping corn

For maple peanut pops

30 g (1 oz) butter

45 g (1½ oz)
crunchy peanut butter

1 tablespoon
maple syrup

For cheesy pops

30 g (1 oz) butter

30 g (1 oz) grated
Parmesan cheese

½ teaspoon salt

Popping the corn

1 Heat the vegetable oil in a large saucepan until hot. Add the popping corn, spreading it out to cover the base of the pan.

2 Cook the corn until it starts to pop, then put on the lid. Cook it for 3 more minutes, while shaking the pan.

Maple peanut pops

Melt the butter, peanut butter, and syrup in a small saucepan over a low heat. Stir it well, then pour it over the popcorn.

Cheesy pops

Melt the butter in a small pan over a low heat. Stir in the grated cheese and salt. Spoon over the popcorn and mix well.

Maple peanut pops

Cheesy pops

CHUNKY CHIPS

You will need

Small kitchen brush
Chopping board • Sharp knife
Small bowl • Pastry brush
Baking sheet

Ingredients

450 g (1 lb) potatoes

4-5 tablespoons sunflower or olive oil

Salt and pepper

Tasty tips

• To give a Mediterranean flavour to the chips, sprinkle them with dried mixed herbs before cooking them.

• Make delicious parsnip chips by cooking parsnips in the same way as the potatoes.

What to do

1 Set the oven. Scrub the potatoes until clean. Cut them in half lengthwise, then cut them into narrow wedges.

2 Brush the baking sheet with oil. Lay the potato wedges in one layer on top, then brush them with oil and *season*.

Mayonnaise for dipping

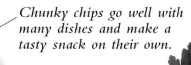

3 *Bake* the potato wedges on the top shelf of the oven for about 20 minutes or until crisp, golden brown, and puffy.

Chunky chips go well with many dishes and make a tasty snack on their own.

Tomato ketchup

17

PITTA POCKETS

You will need

Chopping board • Sharp knife
Grill pan • Spoon

Ingredients

1 or 2 pitta breads
per person

Suggested fillings

Hummus

 Sliced cucumber

Sliced pitted black olives

 Sliced red pepper

Lettuce leaves or
shredded lettuce

 Turkish meatballs
(see page 34)

Yogurt and
mint leaves

 Sliced cold chicken

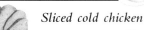 *Guacamole (see page 30)*

What to do

1 Assemble the ingredients for the filling of your choice. *Chop* or *slice* any ingredients that are not ready to use.

2 Heat the pitta breads under the grill for 1 minute on each side, then slit them open and pack with the filling.

To make this pocket, fill it with guacamole and chicken. Tomato can be added for extra colour.

The filling in this pocket is shredded lettuce, sliced meatballs, and a dollop of yogurt mixed with chopped mint.

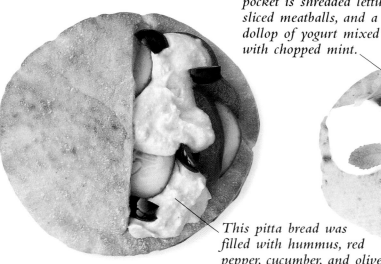

This pitta bread was filled with hummus, red pepper, cucumber, and olives.

CHEATS' PIZZAS

You will need

Grill pan • Chopping board
Bread knife • Spoon

Ingredients

 1 muffin per person

 Tomato passata or sauce

Suggested toppings

Mozzarella cheese

Grated Cheddar cheese

Freshly grated Parmesan cheese

Sliced pepperoni

Strips of ham

Drained tinned tuna

Sliced mushrooms

Sliced pitted olives

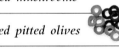 *Finely sliced red pepper*

Sliced tomato

What to do

1 Heat the grill and toast the muffins for 1 to 2 minutes on each side. Slice the muffins in half with a bread knife.

2 Put a spoonful of tomato passata or tomato sauce on each muffin, then spread it evenly across the top.

3 Layer on the toppings you like best, then *grill* the pizzas for a few more minutes until the cheese is melted and bubbly.

To make a tuna pizza, top the muffin with sliced mozzarella, tuna fish, tomato, and black olives.

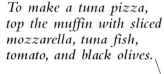

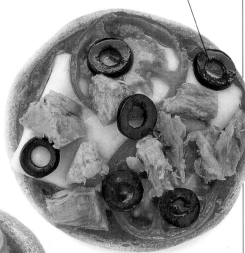

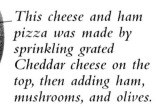

Make a pepperoni pizza using sliced mozzarella, red pepper, pepperoni, and olives.

This cheese and ham pizza was made by sprinkling grated Cheddar cheese on the top, then adding ham, mushrooms, and olives.

HOT DOGS WITH SALSA

You will need

Large saucepan • Colander • Chopping board • Bread knife • Sharp knife Spoon • Bowl • Lemon squeezer

For the hot dogs

4 Frankfurter sausages

4 hot-dog rolls

For the salsa

½ small onion

225 g (8 oz) tomatoes

½ lime

A few drops Tabasco sauce

Salt and pepper

Making the hot dogs

1 Heat a large saucepan of water until it *simmers*, then add the sausages. Cook them for 5 minutes, then drain them.

2 Warm the rolls in the oven for a few minutes, then split each one down the middle. Put a cooked sausage in each roll.

Making the salsa

1 *Chop* the onion finely. Cut the tomatoes in half, then scoop out and discard the seeds. Chop the tomato flesh finely.

2 Put the chopped tomato in a bowl. Add the onion, the juice of half a lime, the Tabasco, and the *seasoning* and mix well.

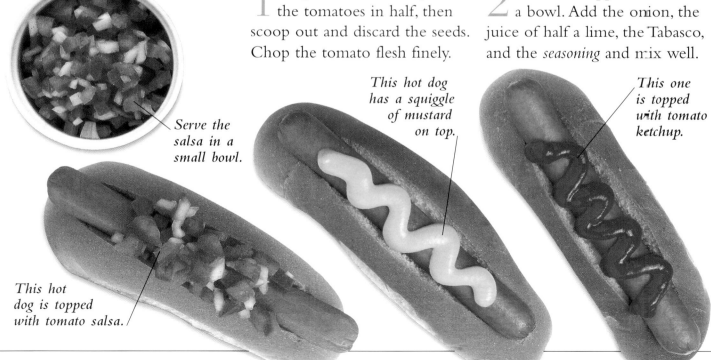

Serve the salsa in a small bowl.

This hot dog is topped with tomato salsa.

This hot dog has a squiggle of mustard on top.

This one is topped with tomato ketchup.

COOL CATS

You will need

Chopping board • Bread knife
Shallow plate • Spoon • Frying pan
Fish slice • Grill pan • Knife

Ingredients

4 thick slices of large French bread stick

55 g (2 oz) plain flour

Salt and pepper

4 flat, skinned and boned fillets of fish

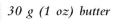

1 tablespoon vegetable oil

30 g (1 oz) butter

Butter for spreading

½ lemon

What to do

1 Turn on the grill. Cut each slice of bread in half. Put the flour on a shallow plate and *season* it with salt and pepper.

2 One at a time, lay each fillet of fish in the seasoned flour, turning it over so that it is coated with flour on both sides.

3 Heat the oil and butter in a frying pan. When they are hot, *fry* the fish for about 3 minutes on each side.

4 Warm the bread under the grill, then butter it. Sandwich each piece of fish in two slices of bread. Add a dash of lemon juice.

Tomato ketchup

Mayonnaise

Serve the cool cats with wedges of lemon.

The flour gives the fish a crispy coating.

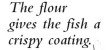

FRUIT SMOOTHIES

You will need

Chopping board • Sharp knife
Blender or food processor • 2 glasses

Ingredients

175 g (6 oz) strawberries	
1 banana	
1 lemon	
1 tablespoon caster sugar	
115 g (4 oz) natural yogurt	
150 ml (¼ pint) milk	

What to do

1 Wipe the strawberries and remove their stalks. Peel and slice the banana and put it in the blender with a squeeze of lemon.

2 Add the strawberries, sugar, yogurt, and milk. Put the lid on the blender and whizz for 1 minute until smooth and frothy.

Serve the smoothies with colourful drinking straws.

These smoothies are strawberry flavoured. For other flavours, try using raspberries, apricots, or pitted cherries.

ICE-CREAM SODA

You will need

*Glass • Ice-cream scoop
or large spoon*

Ingredients

2 scoops strawberry
or vanilla ice cream

75 ml (2½ fl oz)
strawberry or
lime cordial

1 bottle soda water,
fizzy lemonade, or cola

What to do

1 Put 2 scoops of strawberry
or vanilla ice cream into a
tall glass, then pour strawberry
or lime cordial over the top.

2 Slowly pour enough soda
water, lemonade, or cola on
top of the ice cream and cordial
to fill the drinking glass.

*Strawberry soda made
with strawberry
ice cream,
strawberry cordial,
and soda water.*

*Lime soda made
with vanilla ice
cream, lime cordial,
and lemonade.*

SUNSHINE TOAST

You will need

*Chopping board • Biscuit cutter
Small bowl • Frying pan • Fish slice*

Ingredients

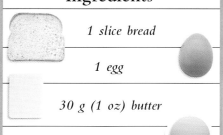

1 slice bread

1 egg

30 g (1 oz) butter

1 tablespoon vegetable oil

What to do

1 Lay the slice of bread down flat and cut a hole in the middle of it with a biscuit cutter. Break the egg into a small bowl.

2 Heat the butter and oil in a frying pan. When they are hot, put the bread in the frying pan and *fry* it on one side.

3 Turn the slice of bread over with a fish slice, then tip the egg out of the bowl into the hole in the middle of the bread.

4 *Fry* the bread and egg until the egg white is set but the yolk is still runny, then lift it out of the pan on to a plate.

Sunshine toast makes a delicious breakfast on its own or with grilled bacon and tomatoes.

Speedy Meals

SPEEDY CHEESY OMELETTE

You will need

Bowl • Whisk or fork • Non-stick frying pan • Fish slice • Plate

Ingredients

2 eggs

Salt and pepper

A knob of butter

1 tablespoon grated cheese

Chopped fresh parsley for garnish (optional)

Tasty tips

You can vary the basic omelette recipe by using different fillings.

• To make a ham omelette, use 1 tablespoon of cooked diced ham or bacon instead of cheese.

• To make a herb omelette, use 1 tablespoon chopped fresh parsley and chives instead of cheese.

What to do

1 Break the eggs into a bowl. Add a little salt and pepper, and *beat* the eggs lightly with a whisk or fork until frothy.

2 Melt the butter in a frying pan. When it begins to foam, pour in the eggs, then sprinkle the cheese on top.

3 As the edges of the omelette set, lift them gently and tilt the pan so that the runny egg flows underneath and cooks.

4 When the top has set but is still creamy, loosen the edges of the omelette and fold it in half. Slip it on to a warm plate.

Omelette made with chopped ham

Speedy cheesy omelette

Herb omelette flavoured with parsley and chives

SPANISH OMELETTE

You will need

*Chopping board • Sharp knife
Non-stick frying pan
Wooden spoon • Mixing bowl
Whisk or fork • Fish slice*

Ingredients

 1 large onion

1 large red pepper

2 medium-sized cooked potatoes

2 tablespoons sunflower oil

4 eggs

Salt and pepper

30 g (1 oz) butter

Tasty tips

For a change, try adding other ingredients to the omelette, such as 115 g (4 oz) cooked spicy sausage cut into chunks, or 115 g (4 oz) diced smoked ham.

What to do

1 Peel the onion and *chop* it finely. *Slice* the potatoes. Cut the pepper in half, remove the seeds, and *dice* it.

2 Heat the oil in a frying pan. Cook the onion and pepper gently until soft. Add the potato and cook for 2 minutes.

3 *Beat* the eggs in a bowl. Stir in the onions, peppers, and potatoes, and *season*. Melt the butter in the frying pan.

4 Pour the mixture into the pan. Cook over a low heat for about 10 minutes, then finish cooking the top under the grill.

This omelette is delicious served cold at a picnic.

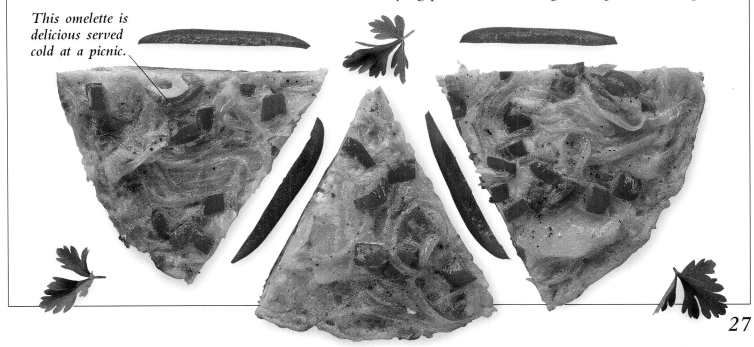

PEA SOUP

You will need

Chopping board • Sharp knife
Large saucepan • Wooden spoon
Spoon • Blender or food processor

Ingredients

4 spring onions

55 g (2 oz) butter

450 ml (¾ pint) water

450 g (1 lb) frozen peas

300 ml (½ pint) single cream or milk

2 teaspoons chopped mint or chives

Salt and pepper

What to do

1 Trim the spring onions and *slice* them finely. Melt the butter in a saucepan. Cook the onions over a low heat until soft.

2 Add the water. Bring it to the *boil*, then add the peas. *Simmer* for 3 to 4 minutes until the peas are tender.

You can serve the soup with a swirl of cream in the middle.

3 Let the soup cool for a few minutes, then pour it into a blender. Put on the lid and whizz until the soup is smooth.

4 Return the soup to the saucepan and stir in the cream and chopped mint or chives. *Season* and reheat gently.

CARROT AND ORANGE SOUP

You will need

*Chopping board • Potato peeler
Sharp knife • Zester or grater • Lemon
squeezer • Large saucepan with lid
Blender or food processor • Wooden spoon*

Ingredients

675 g (1½ lb) carrots

2 cloves garlic

1 orange

1 lemon

300 ml (½ pint) water

Large pinch ground nutmeg

300 ml (½ pint) orange juice

300 ml (½ pint) single cream

Salt and pepper

What to do

1 Peel and *slice* the carrots. Peel the garlic, peel or grate the zest of the orange, and squeeze the juice from the lemon.

2 Put the carrots, garlic, zest, orange juice, and water in a pan. Cover and *simmer* for 20 minutes until the carrots are soft.

Garnish the soup with a sprig of parsley or a little grated orange zest.

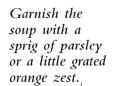

3 Let the soup cool for a few minutes. Add the nutmeg and lemon juice. Pour it into a blender and whizz until smooth.

4 Return the soup to the pan, stir in the cream, and add the *seasoning*. Then reheat the soup without letting it *boil*.

TACOS AND GUACAMOLE

You will need

Chopping board • Sharp knife
Garlic press • Large saucepan
Wooden spoon • Baking tray
Spoon • Mixing bowl
Fork • Lemon squeezer

Ingredients

8 taco shells
for each filling

For a meat filling

 1 onion

1 clove garlic

2 tablespoons vegetable oil

 450 g (1 lb)
minced beef

1 teaspoon ground cinnamon

½ teaspoon mild chilli powder

Salt, pepper, and pinch of oregano

For a bean filling

 1 onion

1 carrot

 1 clove garlic

2 tablespoons vegetable oil

Salt and pepper

Pinch of cayenne pepper

½ teaspoon mild chilli powder

½ teaspoon chilli sauce

Squeeze of lemon

400 g (14 oz) tinned
chopped tomatoes

 450 g (1 lb) tinned
red kidney beans

For the guacamole

2 large, ripe avocados

1 lime

A few drops chilli sauce

Salt and pepper

Making a meat filling

1 Set the oven. *Chop* the onion and crush the garlic. Heat the oil in a saucepan, then cook the onion and garlic until soft.

2 Add the meat. Stir it and cook until brown. Add the oregano, salt, pepper, and spices and cook over a low heat for 10 minutes.

Making a bean filling

1 *Chop* the onion, *dice* the carrot, and crush the garlic. Heat the oil, then cook the vegetables until soft, *season* and stir in the dry spices.

2 Stir in the tomatoes, beans, chilli sauce, and lemon juice. Cook gently for 15 minutes, or until the sauce has thickened.

Filling the tacos

1 Stand the tacos, open side down, on a baking tray. Put them in the oven for about 3 minutes to warm up.

2 Spoon one of the fillings into the warm taco shells, then garnish with toppings, such as shredded lettuce and grated cheese.

Making the guacamole

1 Cut each avocado in half around its stone, then scoop out the stone with a spoon and peel away the skin.

2 Cut up the avocado flesh and put it into a bowl. Then mash it with a fork to make a smooth, thick paste.

3 Squeeze the lime. Add the lime juice, chilli sauce, salt, and pepper to the avocado. Mix everything together until smooth.

Taco toppings

Serve the tacos with small bowls of guacamole, soured cream, and tomato relish for people to add as extra toppings.

Guacamole

Bean-filled taco garnished with shredded lettuce and grated cheese

Soured cream

Meat-filled taco with spring onion, cheese, and lettuce

Tomato relish

PERFECT PASTA

You will need

Chopping board • Sharp knife • Garlic press • Frying pan • Wooden spoon Large saucepan • Colander • Fork Grill pan • Grater • Baking dish

Ingredients

 1 onion

 1 clove garlic

2 tablespoons olive oil

 400 g (14 oz) tinned tomatoes

1 tablespoon tomato purée

Salt and pepper

Pinch of sugar

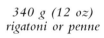 340 g (12 oz) rigatoni or penne

 450 g (1 lb) favourite sausages

 30 g (1 oz) bread

30 g (1 oz) Cheddar cheese

Tasty tips

• You can vary this recipe by using different pasta shapes. Check the cooking time for the sort you are using on the packet.

• If you are cooking for vegetarians, leave out the sausages and increase the amount of cheese used in the topping to 85 g (3 oz).

What to do

1 Set the oven. Peel the onion and *chop* it finely. Peel the garlic and crush it or chop it finely. Heat the oil in a frying pan.

2 Cook the onion and garlic over a low heat until soft, then add the tinned tomatoes and tomato purée and stir well.

3 Let the pasta sauce *simmer* over a low heat for about 10 minutes. Then *season* it with salt, pepper, and a pinch of sugar.

4 *Boil* some salted water in a saucepan. Add the pasta, cook it for about 12 minutes until just soft, then drain it in a colander.

5 Meanwhile, turn on the grill. Prick the sausages with a fork, then *grill* them on all sides for about 10–12 minutes until brown.

6 Remove the sausages from the grill, leave them until they are cool enough to handle, then cut them into chunky slices.

7 Grate the cheese for the topping. Grate the bread into breadcrumbs or else make the breadcrumbs in a food processor.

8 Stir the cooked pasta and the sliced sausages into the tomato sauce, then spoon the mixture into a baking dish.

9 Sprinkle the breadcrumbs and grated cheese over the pasta. *Bake* for 20 to 25 minutes until the topping is crisp.

Perfect meal

Baked pasta is delicious and very filling, so a simple green salad is all you need to serve with it.

When the pasta is baked, the cheese melts into the breadcrumbs, forming a crisp, golden topping.

Rigatoni and penne are tube-shaped pasta, but you can use any other pasta shape you choose.

TURKISH MEATBALLS

You will need

Chopping board • Sharp knife
Garlic press • Mixing bowl • Wooden
spoon • Bamboo skewers • Small bowl
Pastry brush • Grill pan

Ingredients

1 small onion

1 clove garlic

450 g (1 lb) minced lamb

A few fresh mint leaves

1 teaspoon ground allspice

1 teaspoon ground cinnamon

Salt and pepper

Vegetable oil for grilling

Handy hints

To prevent the bamboo
skewers from burning, soak
them in water for about
30 minutes before putting
them under a grill or on
a barbecue.

What to do

1 Peel the onion and *chop* it finely. Peel and crush the garlic. Put the onion, garlic, and minced lamb in a mixing bowl.

2 *Chop* the mint finely. Sprinkle the mint, allspice, cinnamon, salt, and pepper over the lamb and mix it into a paste.

3 Split the mixture into 8 portions and mould them into sausage shapes around the skewers. Brush them with oil.

4 Heat the grill and cook the meatballs for 10 to 12 minutes, turning them regularly until they are brown all over.

Serve the meatballs on a bed of shredded lettuce.

Use parsley leaves as a garnish.

Lemon wedges can be squeezed over the meatballs.

FALAFEL

You will need

Chopping board • Sharp knife • Tea towel
Garlic press • Colander • Large bowl
Fork or food processor • Wooden spoon
Frying pan • Fish slice • Kitchen paper

Ingredients

 1 medium onion

 15 g (½ oz)
flat-leaved parsley

 2 cloves garlic

 800 g (28 oz)
tinned chick peas

2 tablespoons
plain flour

1 teaspoon ground coriander

1 teaspoon ground cumin

 Vegetable oil
for frying

What to do

1 *Chop* the onion finely. Wash, dry, and *chop* the parsley. Peel and crush the garlic and rinse and drain the chick peas.

2 Mash the chick peas with a fork or in a food processor. Mix in the onion, garlic, flour, parsley, coriander, and cumin.

3 With floured hands, roll the mixture into balls about the size of golf balls, then flatten them to make small patties.

4 Heat the oil and *fry* the falafel for a few minutes on each side until golden brown. Drain them on kitchen paper.

Add chopped mint and a dash of cayenne pepper to plain yogurt and serve it with the falafel.

Serve the falafel in warm pitta bread with diced cucumber and tomato.

FISHCAKE FLOUNDERS

You will need

Chopping board • Potato peeler
Sharp knife • Saucepan • Tea towel
Whisk or fork • Small bowl • 3 shallow
bowls or plates • Bowl • Potato masher
Wooden spoon • Frying pan • Fish slice

Ingredients

340 g (12 oz) potatoes

Small bunch parsley

400 g (14 oz)
tinned tuna fish

2 eggs

55 g (2 oz) plain flour

55 g (2 oz) fresh breadcrumbs

Small knob butter

Salt and pepper

Vegetable oil for frying

Tasty tips

Instead of using tuna, you could
make the fishcakes with tinned
salmon. This will give them a
slightly different flavour.

What to do

1 Peel the potatoes, cut them
into large chunks and place in
a saucepan of salted water. *Boil* for
12 to 18 minutes until tender.

2 Meanwhile, wash and dry
the parsley, cut off the stalks
and *chop* the rest finely. Drain off
any liquid from the tuna fish.

3 *Beat* the eggs with a whisk or
fork in a small bowl. Put the
eggs, flour, and breadcrumbs into
3 separate shallow bowls or plates.

4 When the potatoes have
cooked, drain off the water
and mash them. Stir in the butter
and *season* with salt and pepper.

5 Add the tuna fish and the
chopped parsley to the
mashed potatoes, then stir the
mixture together really well.

6 Split the tuna mixture into 4
or 8 portions. Roll each one
into a ball with your hands, then
flatten it into a round fishcake.

7 Turn each fishcake in the
flour to coat it completely,
then dip it in the beaten egg and
finally in the breadcrumbs.

8 Heat the vegetable oil in a frying pan. When it is hot, *fry* the fishcakes on both sides until crisp and golden brown.

Fun fish dish

Using green beans and slices of lemon, you can magically turn fishcakes into funny flounders.

Serve the fishcakes with tomato ketchup.

Green beans steamed until tender look like deep-sea plants.

Make an eye out of a slice of green bean.

Use slices of lemon as fish tails.

CHICKEN NUGGETS

You will need

Grater or food processor • 2 shallow bowls or plates • Bowl • Whisk or fork • Chopping board • Sharp knife • Frying pan • Fish slice

Ingredients

55 g (2 oz) bread

Salt and pepper

2 eggs

4 skinned chicken breasts

2 tablespoons vegetable oil

Mayonnaise for dipping

Tomato ketchup

Use ready-made breadcrumbs for super-fast nuggets.

What to do

1 Grate the bread. Put the crumbs into a shallow bowl and *season*. *Beat* the eggs. Pour them into another shallow bowl.

2 Flatten the chicken breasts with your hands, then carefully cut them into chunks about 2½ cm (1 in) across.

3 Dip the chicken pieces into the egg and turn them to coat them on all sides. Then coat them in the breadcrumbs.

4 Heat the oil in a frying pan and *fry* the nuggets for about 10 minutes, turning them until they are brown on all sides.

LEMONY FISH FINGERS

You will need

Chopping board • Sharp knife • Grater or food processor • Grater or zester Bowl • Whisk or fork • 2 shallow bowls Frying pan • Fish slice

Ingredients

 Small bunch parsley

55 g (2 oz) bread

1 lemon

Salt and pepper

2 eggs

 450 g (1 lb) skinned and boned white fish fillets

 1 tablespoon vegetable oil

 Knob of butter

Tasty tips

If you like dried mixed herbs, add a small pinch to the breadcrumbs in step 1.

What to do

1 *Chop* the parsley. Grate the bread. Peel or grate the zest from the lemon, then mix the 3 ingredients in a bowl and *season*.

2 *Beat* the eggs. Put the eggs and the breadcrumbs into two separate shallow bowls. Cut the fish into finger shapes.

3 Dip the pieces of fish in the beaten egg and then in the breadcrumbs. Make sure each fish finger is coated evenly.

4 Heat the oil and butter in a frying pan. *Fry* the fish fingers for about 4 minutes on each side until crisp and golden.

BARBECUED SPARE RIBS

You will need

*Garlic press • Bowl • Whisk or fork
Shallow dish • Grill pan (if using
grill) • Tongs • Pastry brush
Small saucepan • Wooden spoon*

Ingredients

**12 pork
spare ribs**

For the barbecue sauce

 1 clove garlic

 *2 tablespoons dark brown
muscovado sugar*

*2 tablespoons light
soy sauce*

 *2 tablespoons
tomato purée*

*1 dessertspoon
maple syrup or honey*

½ teaspoon ready-made mustard

Black pepper

What to do

1 Crush the garlic. Put it in
a bowl with the sugar, soy
sauce, tomato purée, maple syrup,
mustard, and pepper. Whisk well.

2 Lay the ribs in a shallow
dish. Pour the sauce over
the ribs, then leave them to
marinate for at least 20 minutes.

3 Heat the grill or barbecue
until hot. *Grill* the ribs for
about 15 minutes on each side.
Brush with sauce if needed.

4 Heat any sauce that is left
over in a saucepan, let it
simmer and serve it with the
barbecued spare ribs.

*Each rib is
coated with
delicious
barbecue
sauce.*

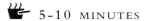
VEGETABLE BARBECUE

You will need

Chopping board • Skewers • Small bowl • Pastry brush • Grill pan (if using grill) • Tongs • Metal skewer (for testing) • Sharp knife

Ingredients

20 cherry tomatoes

2 cobs sweetcorn

Olive oil

Salt and pepper

Tasty tips

You can either grill or barbecue the vegetables. They go well with the barbecued spare ribs on page 40, or with sausages or burgers.

Barbecued sweetcorn

What to do

1 Heat the grill or barbecue. Thread the tomatoes on to skewers. Brush the sweetcorn with olive oil, then *season* it.

2 *Grill* the tomatoes and sweetcorn, turning them so they cook evenly. The tomatoes will take about 5 minutes.

3 When the sweetcorn is golden brown, push a skewer into it to see if it is tender. It should take 5 to 10 minutes.

4 Leave the cooked sweetcorn until it is cool enough to handle, then carefully cut it into chunks about 4 cm (1½ in) wide.

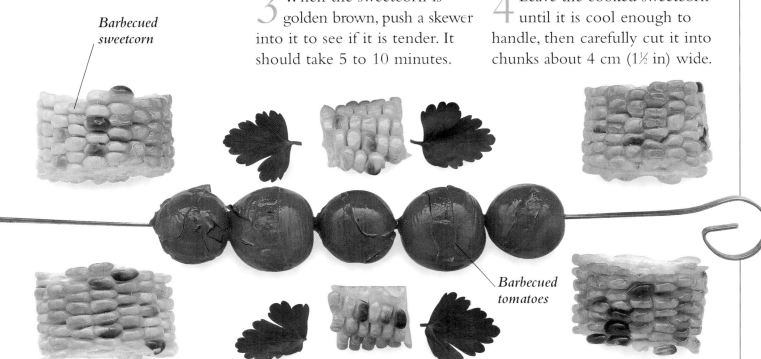

Barbecued tomatoes

CHICKEN CHOW-MEIN

You will need

Large saucepan • Wooden spoon
Colander • Chopping board
Potato peeler • Sharp knife
Grater • Garlic press • Large frying
pan or wok • Lemon squeezer

For the noodles

 225 g (8 oz) dried medium egg noodles

1 teaspoon sunflower oil

For the stir fry

 2 carrots

115 g (4 oz) fine green beans

115 g (4 oz) mangetout

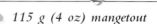 *4 spring onions*

2½ cm (1 in) cube root ginger

1 clove garlic

2 tablespoons sunflower oil

 2 skinless chicken breasts

 1 tablespoon soy sauce

½ lemon

½ teaspoon salt

Tasty tips

• For a change, try steak or pork fillet instead of chicken.

• For vegetarian chow-mein, replace the chicken with 115 g (4 oz) courgettes and 115 g (4 oz) broccoli.

What to do

1 Half-fill a large saucepan with water and bring it to the *boil*. Add the noodles and *boil* them for 4 minutes.

2 Drain the noodles in a colander and rinse them in cold water. Return them to the pan and mix in the sunflower oil.

3 Peel the carrots and cut them into thin sticks. Trim the beans and mangetout. Trim and *slice* the spring onions.

4 Peel the ginger and grate it coarsely. Peel the garlic and either crush it with a garlic press or chop it finely.

5 Heat the oil in a frying pan. Cut the chicken into strips, *stir-fry* it for a few minutes until golden, then leave it on a plate.

6 Put the garlic, ginger, carrots, and beans in the frying pan. *Stir-fry* them for 4 to 5 minutes, turning them all the time.

Soy sauce

7 Add the chicken, mangetout, spring onions, and noodles. Mix everything together and cook for a few more minutes.

8 Add the soy sauce, the juice of half a lemon, and the salt and mix once more. Cook for 2 minutes to heat through.

Noodle feast

Chow-mein is noodles *stir-fried* with lots of tasty vegetables. Try using chopsticks to eat it as the Chinese do!

Chopsticks

CHICKEN CURRY AND RICE

You will need

*Chopping board • Sharp knife
Grater • Large frying pan
with lid • Wooden spoon
Plate • Saucepan with lid*

For the chicken curry

 2½ cm (1 in) cube fresh ginger

 1 onion

 2 cloves garlic

 *4 skinned
chicken breasts*

 2 tablespoons vegetable oil

 *2 tablespoons mild
Madras curry powder*

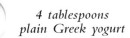 *200 ml (7 fl oz)
chicken stock*

Salt and pepper

 *4 tablespoons
plain Greek yogurt*

1 sprig fresh coriander

For the rice

 1 small onion

30 g (1 oz) butter

1 stick cinnamon

1 teaspoon ground turmeric

 *225 g (8 oz)
long grain rice*

Salt

 *600 ml (1 pint) chicken
or vegetable stock*

Making the chicken curry

1 Cut the peel off the cube of ginger with a sharp knife, then grate the ginger on the coarsest part of the grater.

2 Peel the onion and the garlic, then *chop* them both finely. Carefully cut the chicken into bite-sized pieces.

3 Heat the oil in a frying pan. When hot, cook the chicken pieces quickly on all sides until golden, then move them to a plate.

4 *Fry* the onion and garlic until they turn brown at the edges. Stir in the ginger and curry powder and cook for 1 minute.

5 Add the chicken, then the stock. Put the lid on the frying pan and cook over a low heat for about 20 minutes.

6 Let the curry cool for a few minutes, then stir in the *seasoning* and yogurt. *Chop* the coriander and add it to the curry.

Making the rice

1 *Chop* the onion finely. Melt the butter in a pan and cook the onion until transparent. Add the spices. Cook for 1 minute.

2 Add the rice and salt and stir well. Cook them over a low heat for a few more minutes until the rice looks transparent.

3 Pour on the stock. Put a lid on the pan and *simmer* for 15 to 20 minutes until the rice is tender and has absorbed the stock.

Curry feast

Spread the rice out on a warm serving plate and spoon the chicken curry on top.

THAI KEBABS WITH SATAY SAUCE

You will need

Bamboo skewers • Chopping board
Sharp knife • Bowl • Garlic press
Grater • Whisk • 3 shallow bowls
Saucepan • Wooden spoon • Grill pan

For the kebabs

 1 small pork fillet

 2 small skinless chicken breasts

 12 large cooked, peeled prawns

For the marinade

 2 tablespoons soy sauce

2 tablespoons clear honey

Juice of 1 lime

A few drops Tabasco sauce

 1 clove garlic

1 cm (½ in) cube fresh ginger

For the satay sauce

 ½ onion

1 cm (½ in) cube fresh ginger

 1 clove garlic

1½ tablespoons vegetable oil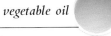

1 dessertspoon soy sauce

3 tablespoons water

 1½ tablespoons light brown sugar

5 tablespoons peanut butter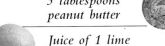

Juice of 1 lime

Salt if needed

Preparing the meat

1 Soak the skewers in water for 30 minutes. Cut the pork into thin diagonal slices, then cut each slice into narrow strips.

2 Flatten the chicken breasts with your hands, then carefully cut them into strips about 2½ cm (1 in) wide.

Making the marinade

1 Put the soy sauce, honey, lime juice, and Tabasco into a bowl. Crush the garlic, peel and grate the ginger, and stir them in.

2 Pour the marinade into 3 bowls. Put the pork, chicken, and prawns into the 3 bowls, turn them, and leave to *marinate*.

Making the satay sauce

1 Peel the onion and *chop* it very finely. Peel the ginger and grate it coarsely, then peel and crush the garlic.

2 Heat the oil in a saucepan. Cook the onion gently until soft. Add the ginger and garlic and cook for a few minutes.

Making the kebabs

3 Put the onion mixture, soy sauce, water, sugar, peanut butter, and lime juice in a bowl and whisk. Add salt if needed.

1 Thread the prawns on to skewers. Fold the strips of pork and chicken and thread them on to separate skewers.

2 *Grill* the pork and chicken for about 4 minutes on each side until brown. *Grill* the prawns for about 1 minute on each side.

Thai treat
Serve the kebabs with wedges of fresh lime and a bowl of satay sauce.

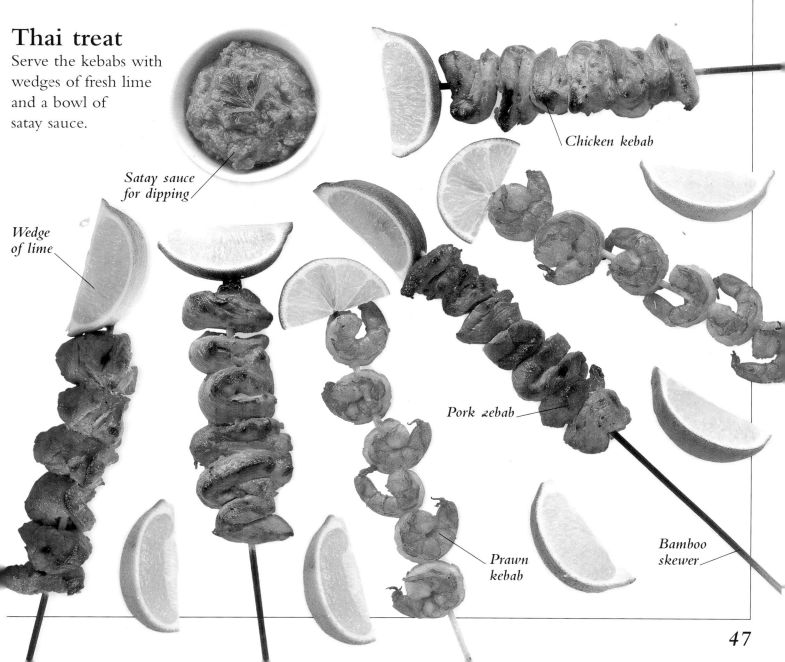

Satay sauce for dipping

Chicken kebab

Wedge of lime

Pork kebab

Prawn kebab

Bamboo skewer

SALADE NIÇOISE

You will need

Chopping board • Potato peeler
Sharp knife • 3 saucepans
Colander or sieve • Bowl • Tea towel
Screw-top jar • Salad bowl

For the salad

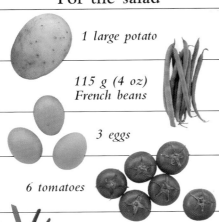

1 large potato

115 g (4 oz)
French beans

3 eggs

6 tomatoes

3 spring onions

30 g (1 oz) parsley

1 crisp lettuce

400 g (14 oz)
tinned tuna fish

6 anchovy
fillets

85 g (3 oz) pitted
black olives

For the dressing

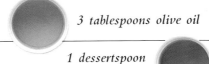

3 tablespoons olive oil

1 dessertspoon
wine vinegar

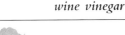

½ teaspoon French mustard

Salt and pepper

What to do

1 Peel the potato and cut it into bite-sized chunks. *Boil* the potato until tender, drain it, and leave to cool.

2 Trim the beans, then cook them in a saucepan of *boiling* water for 5 minutes until tender. Rinse them under a cold tap.

3 *Boil* the eggs for 10 minutes, then put them in a bowl of cold water to cool. Shell the eggs and cut them into quarters.

4 Cut up the tomatoes. Rinse and dry the parsley, cut off the stalks, and *chop* the leaves finely. *Slice* the spring onions.

5 Put the olive oil, vinegar, mustard, salt, and pepper into a jar. Screw on the lid and shake well to make the dressing.

6 Rinse the lettuce leaves in a bowl of cold water, drain them, then pat them dry. Line a salad bowl with the leaves.

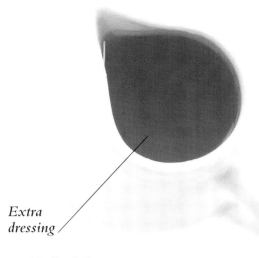

7 Arrange the potatoes, tuna, tomatoes, onions, beans, eggs, and parsley on top of the lettuce and sprinkle on some dressing.

8 Drain the anchovies and cut them in half lengthwise. Lay them on top of the salad and garnish with the olives.

Extra dressing

Mouthwatering salad

To make a light meal, serve the salad with warm, crusty French bread. Pour any left-over salad dressing into a jug and serve it separately.

Arrange the anchovies in a criss-cross pattern.

TABBOULEH

You will need

2 large bowls • Chopping board
Sharp knife • Tea towel
Large sieve • Salad bowl
Wooden spoon

Ingredients

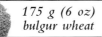
175 g (6 oz) bulgur wheat

½ cucumber

4 spring onions

55 g (2 oz) parsley

30 g (1 oz) fresh mint leaves

3 tablespoons olive oil

3 tablespoons lemon juice

Salt and pepper

Tasty tips

For extra colour, add 3 seeded, diced tomatoes and a handful of pitted black olives.

What to do

1 Put the bulgur wheat in a bowl, cover it with *boiling* water and leave to soak for 20 minutes until the grains soften.

2 Finely *chop* the cucumber. Trim the spring onions and *slice* them finely. Rinse, dry, and finely *chop* the parsley and mint.

3 Drain the bulgur wheat in a sieve over a bowl. Use your hands to squeeze out as much extra water as you can.

4 Put all the ingredients for the tabbouleh into a salad bowl. Mix everything together and *season* with salt and pepper.

Garnish the tabbouleh with sprigs of mint and serve it with slices of lemon.

CARROT SALAD

You will need

Chopping board • Kitchen brush or potato peeler • Grater • Baking sheet Lemon squeezer • Small jar with lid Salad bowl with servers

For the salad

6 large carrots

1 tablespoon sunflower seeds

85 g (3 oz) raisins

For the dressing

½ orange

½ lemon

1 teaspoon clear honey

3 tablespoons hazelnut or olive oil

¼ teaspoon ready-made French mustard

Salt and pepper

Decorate the salad by sprinkling a few extra raisins and sunflower seeds over the top.

What to do

1 Scrub or peel the carrots, then grate them coarsely. Toast the sunflower seeds lightly under the grill for a few minutes.

2 Squeeze the juice out of the orange and lemon. Put the dressing ingredients into a jar, screw on the lid and shake well.

3 Put the carrot, sunflower seeds, and raisins into a salad bowl. Pour the dressing over the top, and toss the salad.

SAVOURY PANCAKES

You will need

Bowl • Whisk • Measuring jug
18 cm (7 in) frying pan • Pastry
brush • Fish slice • Warm plate
Chopping board • Grater
Sharp knife • Wooden spoon • Spoon

For the pancakes

55 g (2 oz) plain flour

55 g (2 oz)
wholewheat flour

Pinch of salt

2 eggs

200 ml (8 fl oz) milk

100 ml (4 fl oz) water

4 tablespoons melted butter

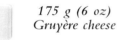

Cheesy filling

175 g (6 oz)
Gruyère cheese

175 g (6 oz)

Mushroom filling

225 g (8 oz) mushrooms

55 g (2 oz) butter

Pinch of flour

Pinch of grated nutmeg

Salt and pepper

4 tablespoons double
or soured cream

What to do

1 Put all the flour and salt in a bowl. Add the eggs and some of the milk and water, whisking them into the flour a bit at a time.

2 Gradually pour the rest of the milk and water into the mixture, whisking until everything is mixed evenly.

3 Add half the melted butter to the mixture and whisk it again to make the finished batter. Pour it into a measuring jug.

4 Brush a frying pan with melted butter and heat until it sizzles. Then pour in 2 tablespoons of pancake batter.

5 Quickly tilt the pan from side to side, so that the base of the frying pan is covered completely with a thin layer of batter.

6 Cook the pancake for about 1 minute, then flip it over and cook it for 10 more seconds. Slide it on to a warm plate.

Cheesy filling

Grate the cheese and *dice* the ham, then mix them together. Sprinkle some of the mixture on to each pancake and fold it over.

Mushroom filling

1 Wipe and finely chop the mushrooms. Melt the butter in a pan and *fry* the mushrooms for a few minutes until tender.

2 Add the flour and *seasoning*. Stir for a minute, then add the cream. Spoon a little filling on to each pancake and fold it over.

Savour the flavour

These savoury pancakes make a delicious light lunch or tea.

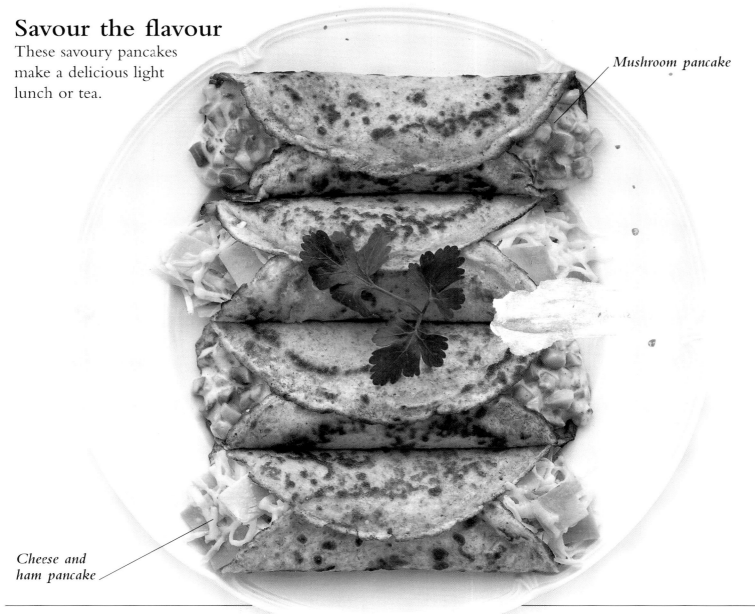

Mushroom pancake

Cheese and ham pancake

SPICY CHICKEN BURGERS

You will need

Chopping board
Sharp knife • Plastic bag
Frying pan • Fish slice
Bread knife • Spoon

For the chicken filling

 2 large, skinned chicken breasts

 55 g (2 oz) plain flour

¼ teaspoon chilli powder

Salt and pepper

 Vegetable oil for frying

For the buns

4 sesame-seed hamburger buns

 Shredded lettuce

Soured cream

Tomato relish or sliced tomato

What to do

1 Carefully cut the chicken breasts in half. Flatten them out by pressing them firmly with the palm of your hand.

2 Put the flour, chilli powder, salt, pepper, and chicken in a plastic bag. Fold over the top of the bag and shake it well.

3 Heat the oil in a frying pan until hot. *Fry* the chicken for about 8 minutes on each side until firm and golden brown.

4 Cut the rolls in half. Fill each one with lettuce, a piece of chicken, soured cream, and tomato relish or sliced tomato.

Nice spice

Chilli powder and soured cream give these burgers a great Tex–Mex flavour.

Tomato relish

Soured cream

Spicy chicken

Shredded lettuce

Sliced tomato

PERFECT
PUDDINGS

PROFITEROLES

You will need

Baking sheet • Sharp knife • Saucepan
Sieve • Greaseproof paper • Wooden spoon
Whisk or fork • 2 teaspoons • Wire rack
Bowl • Whisk or electric mixer

For the profiteroles

Butter for greasing baking sheet

55 g (2 oz) butter

150 ml (¼ pint) water

*70 g (2½ oz)
plain flour*

1 teaspoon caster sugar

 2 eggs

For the sauce

 *115 g (4 oz)
dark chocolate*

30 g (1 oz) butter

4 tablespoons double cream

For the filling

*150 ml (¼ pint)
double cream*

Tasty tips

You can use this recipe to make
chocolate éclairs. Fill a piping bag
with the profiterole mixture and
pipe short fingers on to a baking
sheet. Bake in the same way as the
profiteroles. Fill with cream
and top with chocolate sauce.

What to do

1 Set the oven. *Grease* a baking
sheet and dampen it with
water. Cut up the butter and heat
it in a saucepan with the water.

2 *Sift* the flour and sugar on
to greaseproof paper. When
the water *boils*, remove it from the
heat and tip in the flour and sugar.

3 *Beat* the mixture hard with
a wooden spoon until it is
smooth and comes away from
the sides of the saucepan.

4 *Beat* the eggs, then *beat* them
into the mixture, a little at a
time, until you have a thick,
smooth, glossy paste.

5 Put teaspoons of the mixture
on to the baking sheet. *Bake*
for 20 to 25 minutes until puffy
and golden brown.

6 Put the profiteroles on a wire
rack to cool. Pierce them with
a fork to let out any steam and to
stop them going soft.

7 Break the chocolate into a saucepan. Add the butter and cream. Stir over a low heat until the chocolate has melted.

8 Whisk the cream for the filling in a bowl until thick. Slice open each profiterole and fill with a teaspoon of cream.

9 Arrange the profiteroles on a serving plate. Pour over the chocolate sauce, making sure each profiterole is lightly coated.

Chocolate feast

Pour any extra chocolate sauce into a jug and serve it with the profiteroles.

Eat the profiteroles as soon as you can as they taste best when they're fresh.

15-20 MINUTES　　3-5 MINUTES　　6-8 PEOPLE　　230°C/450°F/GAS MARK 8

BAKED ALASKA

You will need

Baking sheet • Spoon or knife
Big spoon or ice-cream scoop
Palette knife • Mixing bowl
Whisk or electric mixer

Ingredients

20 cm (8 in) sponge
flan case or 6-7 slices
of sponge cake

2 tablespoons
strawberry jam

500 ml (1 pint)
strawberry ice cream

3 egg whites

Pinch of salt

175 g (6 oz)
caster sugar

Tasty tips

Instead of using jam you could
cover the sponge with sliced
strawberries or other fresh fruit.
You can use whichever flavour
ice cream you like.

What to do

1 Set the oven. Put the sponge
flan case or slices of sponge
on the baking sheet and spread
the jam evenly on top.

2 Pile the ice cream on to the
sponge and smooth it into a
rounded shape with a knife. Put
it in the freezer until needed.

3 Put the egg whites and salt
in a bowl and *whisk* them
until they form stiff peaks. Whisk
in the sugar, a little at a time.

4 Quickly cover the flan case
and ice cream with the egg
white. *Bake* for 3 to 5 minutes
until the meringue is pale golden.

*Make peaks in the
meringue before
cooking it.*

KNICKERBOCKER GLORIES

You will need

Chopping board • Sharp knife
Tall glass • Spoon or ice-cream scoop
Piping bag or spoon
Long-handled spoon

For the strawberry glory

 55 g (2 oz) strawberries

3 scoops
strawberry ice cream

Strawberry-flavoured syrup

 1 tablespoon
whipped cream

1 dessertspoon toasted
flaked almonds

For the banoffee glory

 1 banana

3 scoops toffee or
butterscotch ice cream

Maple syrup

 1 tablespoon
whipped cream

1 dessertspoon chopped
pecan nuts or walnuts

*Serve each glory with
a long-handled spoon*

*Strawberry
glory*

*Banoffee
glory*

What to do

1 Wipe the strawberries and
remove the stalks. Slice the
fruit. If making a banoffee glory,
peel and slice the banana.

2 Put layers of ice cream and
sliced fruit in a tall glass.
When the glass is nearly full,
pour a little syrup over the top.

3 Pipe or spoon whipped
cream on top of the ice
cream and fruit, then sprinkle
with the nuts.

LEMON CHEESECAKE

You will need

Plastic bag • Rolling pin • Saucepan
Wooden spoon • 20 cm (8 in)
cake tin (preferably spring-release)
Zester or grater • Lemon squeezer
2 large bowls • Whisk or electric mixer
Metal spoon • Plate

For the base

*175 g (6 oz) any sweet
wholemeal biscuit*

70 g (2½ oz) butter

Butter for greasing cake tin

For the filling

1 lemon

2 eggs

*340 g (12 oz)
mascarpone or other
cream cheese*

*115 g (4 oz)
fromage frais or
soured cream*

85 g (3 oz) caster sugar

1 tablespoon cornflour

For the decoration

Strips of orange and lemon zest

Tasty tips

Orange cheesecake is
also delicious and easy to
make. Just replace the lemon
zest and lemon juice with
the grated zest and juice of
an orange.

What to do

1 Set the oven. Break the biscuits into a large plastic bag and crush them with a rolling pin to make them into crumbs.

2 Melt the butter in a saucepan over a low heat. Turn off the heat and stir the biscuit crumbs into the butter.

3 *Grease* the cake tin. Tip in the biscuit crumbs and press them down evenly to make a base. Now make the filling.

4 Peel or grate the zest from the lemon. Cut the lemon in half and squeeze out the juice. *Separate* the eggs into two bowls.

5 Whisk the lemon zest, lemon juice, egg yolks, mascarpone, fromage frais, sugar, and cornflour in a bowl until smooth.

6 Wash and dry the whisk or electric mixer, then *whisk* the egg whites in a separate bowl until they are stiff and form peaks.

7 Add the whisked egg whites to the cheese mixture. *Fold* them in gently with a metal spoon until they are well mixed.

8 Spoon the filling on to the base and *bake* for 50 minutes. Turn off the oven and leave the cheesecake to cool in the oven.

9 Take the cheesecake out of the oven, remove it from the tin and put it on a plate. Chill it in the fridge overnight, if possible.

Tangy cheesecake

Lemon cheesecake is so delicious and rich, it is best served on its own.

Decorate the cheesecake with fine strips of orange and lemon zest.

TIRAMISU

You will need

Grater or food processor
Mixing bowl • Whisk • Shallow dish
4 individual glasses or 1 glass serving
bowl • Spoon • Teaspoon

Ingredients

 55 g (2 oz) dark chocolate

 225 g (8 oz) mascarpone

225 g (8 oz) fromage frais

55 g (2 oz) caster sugar

 300 ml (½ pint) strong coffee

20 sponge fingers

What to do

1 Grate the chocolate with a grater or in a food processor. Whisk the two cream cheeses and the sugar together in a bowl.

2 Pour the coffee into a dish. Break the sponge fingers in half, dip them in the coffee, and put a layer in each glass.

3 Cover the sponge fingers with a layer of cream cheese and sprinkle with a little of the grated chocolate.

4 Repeat the layers, finishing with cream cheese. Sprinkle this with chocolate and chill in the fridge for 2 to 3 hours.

Chilling the tiramisu helps the flavours of the coffee, cream cheese, and chocolate to blend together.

CLAFOUTI

You will need

23 cm (9 in) ovenproof dish or ceramic flan dish • Chopping board Sharp knife • Saucepan • Mixing bowl • Wooden spoon or whisk Small sieve or tea-strainer

Ingredients

Butter for greasing ovenproof dish

565 g (1¼ lb) plums

45 g (1½ oz) butter

3 large eggs

85 g (3 oz) caster sugar

100 ml (4 fl oz) single cream

85 g (3 oz) plain flour or ground almonds

Icing sugar

Tasty tips

You can also make clafouti with cherries, apricots, apples, greengages, or pears.

What to do

1 Set the oven and *grease* an ovenproof dish. Cut the plums in half and *stone* them. Cut each plum half in two.

2 Melt the butter in a pan. In a bowl, *beat* together the melted butter, eggs, sugar, cream, and flour or ground almonds.

3 Pour the mixture into the ovenproof dish and arrange the quartered plums in a pretty pattern on top of it.

4 Cook the pudding for 40 to 45 minutes until set in the centre. Let it cool a little, then sprinkle with icing sugar.

Clafouti is delicious when it has cooled a little but is still warm. Serve it with single cream.

FRUIT CRUMBLE

You will need

Pie dish • Chopping board • Potato peeler • Sharp knife • Saucepan Wooden spoon • Mixing bowl • Spoon

For the filling

Butter for greasing pie dish

 675 g (1½ lb) cooking apples

30 g (1 oz) soft brown sugar

1 teaspoon cinnamon

 2 tablespoons apple juice

225 g (8 oz) blackberries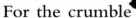

For the crumble

115 g (4 oz) butter

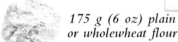 175 g (6 oz) plain or wholewheat flour

55g (2 oz) porridge oats

 85 g (3 oz) soft brown sugar

Pinch of salt

Tasty tips

You can use apricots, plums, or raspberries instead of blackberries in the crumble.

What to do

1 Set the oven. *Grease* the pie dish. Peel the apples, cut them into quarters and cut out the cores, then slice them.

2 Cook the apples, sugar, cinnamon, and apple juice gently in a saucepan until the apples are soft, but not pulpy.

3 Meanwhile *rub* the butter and flour together in a mixing bowl, then mix in the oats, sugar, and salt.

4 Put the apples into the dish and mix in the blackberries. Spread the crumble on top and *bake* for 30 to 40 minutes.

You can serve fruit crumble hot or cold. It is delicious with a scoop of vanilla ice cream.

FRUIT SALAD

You will need

Chopping board • Sharp knife
Glass or china bowl
Large spoon

Ingredients

450 g (1 lb)
fresh pineapple or
tinned pineapple rings

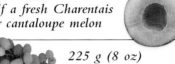

Half a fresh Charentais
or cantaloupe melon

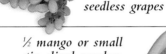

225 g (8 oz)
seedless grapes

½ mango or small
tin sliced peaches

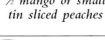

100 ml (4 fl oz)
pineapple juice

Tasty tips

You can make fruit salad
with any fruit you like: try
strawberries, raspberries,
cherries, and sliced banana.

Decorate the
fruit salad with
a sprig of mint.

What to do

1 Cut up the pineapple. Cut the melon into slices, remove the seeds and skin, then cut the slices into chunks.

2 Wash the grapes and cut them in half. Score the flesh of the mango as shown, then slice the chunks away from the skin.

3 Put all the fruit in the bowl, pour the pineapple juice on top, and stir everything together. Chill until needed.

HOT CHOCOLATE PUDS

You will need

*3 bowls • Saucepan
Wooden spoon • 4 ramekins • Whisk
or electric mixer • Large metal spoon
Small sieve or tea-strainer*

Ingredients

*115 g (4 oz)
fine dark chocolate*

*Butter for greasing
ramekins*

55 g (2 oz) caster sugar

5 eggs

Pinch of salt

Icing sugar

What to do

1 Set the oven. Break the chocolate into a bowl. Melt it over a saucepan of *simmering* water, stirring until smooth.

2 Remove the chocolate from the heat. *Grease* the four ramekins lightly and sprinkle with a little of the caster sugar.

3 *Separate* the eggs into two bowls. Stir the rest of the caster sugar and four of the egg yolks into the melted chocolate.

4 *Whisk* all five egg whites with a pinch of salt until they form stiff peaks. Then *fold* them gently into the chocolate.

5 Fill the ramekins until they are nearly full. *Bake* for 15 minutes until the puds rise and puff up. Sprinkle with icing sugar.

Serve the puds straight away.

RASPBERRY FOOLS

You will need

2 bowls • Fork • Large metal spoon
Whisk or electric mixer • 4 ramekins

Ingredients

 285 g (10 oz) raspberries

1 teaspoon lemon juice

30 g (1 oz) caster sugar

150 ml (¼ pint) double cream

140 g (5 oz) fromage frais

Tasty tips

Try making the fool with other types of soft fruit. Leave out the lemon juice and sugar. Once you have made the fool, taste it and add sugar if necessary.

What to do

1 Set aside eight raspberries. Crush the rest with a fork leaving them a little lumpy. Stir in the lemon juice and sugar.

2 Pour the double cream into another bowl and *beat* it with a whisk or electric mixer until it has thickened.

Keep the fools chilled until you are ready to serve them.

3 *Fold* the fromage frais and the cream gently into the raspberries, then spoon the fool into the four ramekins.

Decorate the fools with the remaining whole raspberries.

TOTALLY TERRIFIC TRIFLE

You will need

Glass bowl • Spoon • Saucepan
Wooden spoon • Bowl • Whisk or fork
Chopping board • Knife • Colander
Whisk or electric mixer • Palette knife

For the trifle

 Slices of sponge cake or 5 large macaroons

 Apricot or raspberry jam

5 tablespoons fruit juice or cordial

2 firm, ripe bananas

 400 g (14 oz) tin sliced peaches

For the custard

300 ml (½ pint) double cream

1 teaspoon cornflour

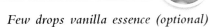 *3 egg yolks*

Few drops vanilla essence (optional)

30 g (1 oz) caster sugar

For the topping

300 ml (½ pint) double cream

 30 g (1 oz) toasted flaked almonds

Handy hints

For a super-speedy trifle, instead of preparing the custard yourself use a 400 g (14 oz) carton of ready-made custard, or make up a packet of instant custard mix.

What to do

1 Break the slices of sponge cake or macaroons into medium-sized pieces and lay them in the bottom of the bowl.

2 Spread a thin layer of jam over the top of the sponge pieces or macaroons, then spoon on enough fruit juice or cordial to soak them.

3 Put the cream for the custard in a saucepan and heat gently until it boils. Whisk the cornflour, eggs, vanilla, and sugar in a bowl.

4 As soon as the cream boils, stir it into the egg mixture a little at a time. Keep stirring the mixture to stop it from curdling.

5 Return the mixture to the pan and stir it over a very low heat until it thickens. Remove from the heat and leave to cool.

6 Peel and slice the bananas and arrange them on top of the jam, then drain the peaches and lay them on top of the bananas.

7 When the custard has cooled completely, carefully spoon it over the layer of peaches, making sure it is spread out evenly.

8 Whip the double cream for the topping with a whisk or electric mixer until it is thick but not completely stiff.

9 Spread the whipped cream over the custard with a palette knife and decorate it with flaked almonds.

Tempting trifle

Creamy, fruity trifle is a good pudding for a party, summer barbecue, or other special occasion.

Decorate the trifle with fresh raspberries.

FRUITY CRÈME BRÛLÉES

You will need

Chopping board • Sharp knife
4 ramekins • Spoon • Knife
Baking sheet or grill pan

Ingredients

175 g (6 oz)
seedless grapes

175 g (6 oz) strawberries

225 g (8 oz)
Greek yogurt

175 g (6 oz) soft brown
sugar or caster sugar

Tasty tips

You can make these tasty puds
with all sorts of fruit: try sliced
banana, mandarin segments, or
your favourite berries.

What to do

1 Wash the grapes. Cut them
in half. Wipe the strawberries
and remove their stalks, then
half fill the ramekins with fruit.

2 Turn the grill on to a high
setting. Cover the fruit with
yogurt, then smooth the top of
the yogurt flat with a knife.

3 Sprinkle enough soft brown
sugar on top of the yogurt
to completely cover it. It should
be at least ½ cm (¼ in) thick.

4 Stand the ramekins on a
baking sheet or grill pan and
put them under the hot grill for a
few minutes until the sugar melts.

Beneath the crunchy
caramel topping is
a creamy mixture
of fruit and yogurt.

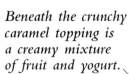

TREATS
AND
SWEETS

ULTIMATE CHOCOLATE CAKE

You will need

20 cm (8 in) cake tin with loose base
Baking parchment • Bowl • Saucepan
Wooden spoon • Knife • 2 large bowls
Whisk or electric mixer • Sieve
Metal spoon • Wire rack • Palette knife

For the cake

Butter for greasing cake tin

175 g (6 oz)
fine dark chocolate

115 g (4 oz) butter

3 tablespoons water

 3 eggs

140 g (5 oz) caster sugar

 85 g (3 oz)
ground almonds

55 g (2 oz)
self-raising flour

Pinch of salt

For the topping

115 g (4 oz)
fine dark chocolate

2 tablespoons soured cream

For the decoration

 Flaked almonds

Tasty tips

• Instead of plain flaked
almonds, you could use
toasted ones for extra flavour.

• You could decorate the cake
with fresh strawberry halves.

Making the cake

1 Set the oven. *Grease* the cake tin, then cut out a circle of baking parchment and *line* the base of the tin with it.

2 Break the chocolate into a bowl. Stand it over a saucepan of *simmering* water and stir until all the chocolate has melted.

3 Cut the butter into small pieces. Add the butter and water to the chocolate and stir until the butter has melted.

4 *Separate* the eggs into two large bowls. Whisk the egg yolks and sugar together until they are thick and creamy.

5 Stir the chocolate mixture into the egg yolk mixture. Add the ground almonds, *sift* in the flour, and mix well.

6 *Whisk* the egg whites with a pinch of salt until they form stiff peaks. *Fold* them gently into the chocolate mixture.

Making the topping

7 Put the mixture into the tin. *Bake* for 40 to 45 minutes. Cool in the tin for 5 minutes, then move to a wire rack.

1 Melt the chocolate in a bowl over a pan of *simmering* water. Remove from the heat and stir in the soured cream.

2 Spread the chocolate topping over the top of the cooled cake with a palette knife, then decorate it with flaked almonds.

Scrumptious cake

When this cake comes out of the oven it has a gooey chocolate centre that sets as it cools.

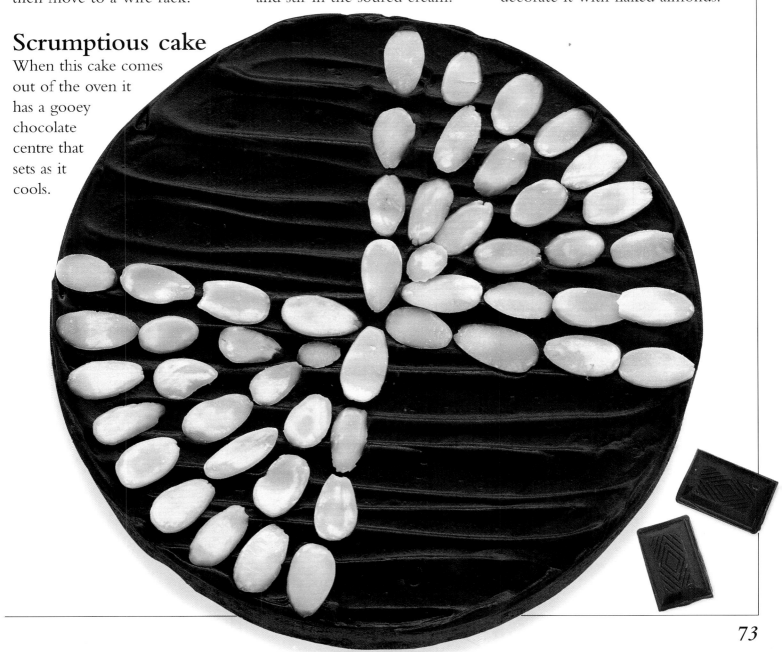

FROSTED CARROT CAKE

You will need

20 cm (8 inch) round cake tin
Baking parchment • Scissors • Sharp knife
Grater or food processor • Sieve • Large
bowl • Wooden spoon • Whisk or fork
Spoon • Skewer • Wire rack • Palette knife

For the cake

Butter for greasing cake tin

225 g (8 oz) carrots

225 g (8 oz) self-raising
flour and 2 teaspoons
baking powder

Pinch of salt

140 g (5 oz) soft brown
muscovado sugar

Grated zest of 1 orange

2 teaspoons ground cinnamon

115 g (4 oz) chopped
roasted hazelnuts
or chopped walnuts

55 g (2 oz) desiccated coconut

2 large eggs

150 ml (¼ pint)
sunflower oil

Juice of 1 orange

For the frosting

225 g (8 oz)
cream cheese

85 g (3 oz) butter

115 g (4 oz)
icing sugar

For the marzipan carrots

225 g (8 oz) marzipan

Orange and green food colouring

Making the cake

1 Set the oven. *Grease* the cake tin. Cut out a circle of baking parchment the same size as the tin and cover the base with it.

2 Scrub or peel the carrots and trim off their tops. Grate the carrots using a grater or a food processor.

3 *Sift* the flour and baking powder into a bowl. Mix in the carrots, salt, sugar, orange zest, cinnamon, nuts, and coconut.

4 *Beat* the eggs. Add the eggs, sunflower oil, and orange juice to the cake mixture and mix everything together well.

5 Spoon the mixture into the cake tin. *Bake* it for 60 to 75 minutes until a skewer pushed into the centre comes out clean.

6 Leave the cake to cool in the tin for 10 to 15 minutes, then remove it from the tin and put it on a wire rack to finish cooling.

Decorating the cake

1 *Beat* the cream cheese, butter, and icing sugar together in a bowl with a wooden spoon until the mixture is soft and creamy.

2 Spread the cream cheese frosting evenly over the top of the cooled cake, using a palette knife dipped in warm water.

3 Knead orange and green food colouring into two balls of marzipan, then mould carrots for the top of the cake.

Teatime special

Spicy carrot cake will stay fresh for several days if you store it in an airtight container.

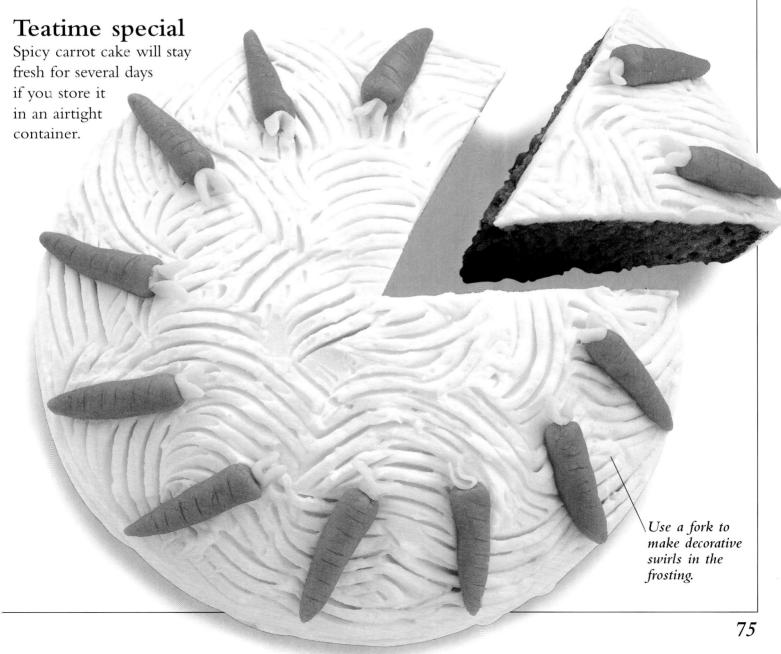

Use a fork to make decorative swirls in the frosting.

MACAROONS

You will need

Baking sheet • Baking parchment
2 bowls • Whisk or electric mixer
Metal spoon • Wire rack

Ingredients

2 medium eggs

175 g (6 oz) ground almonds

175 g (6 oz) caster sugar

What to do

1 Set the oven. Line a baking sheet with baking parchment. *Separate* the egg whites from the yolks and put them in two bowls.

2 Put the yolks in the fridge, as you will not need them. *Whisk* the egg whites until they form stiff peaks.

3 Add the ground almonds and sugar to the egg whites and *fold* them in gently with a metal spoon until well mixed.

4 Roll the mixture into small balls, then put the balls on the baking sheet. *Bake* them for 15 minutes until golden brown.

5 Take the macaroons out of the oven and cool them on a wire rack. Store the macaroons in an airtight container.

Macaroons crack naturally as they cook.

These biscuits are very light and seem to melt in the mouth.

CHOCOLATE MACAROONS

You will need

Baking sheet • Baking parchment
3 bowls • Saucepan • Wooden spoon
Whisk or electric mixer • Metal
spoon • Teaspoon • Wire rack

Ingredients

2 medium eggs

85 g (3 oz) dark chocolate

175 g (6 oz) ground almonds

115 g (4 oz) caster sugar

What to do

1 Set the oven. Line a baking sheet with baking parchment. *Separate* the eggs and put them in two different bowls.

2 Break the chocolate into a bowl and heat it over a pan of *simmering* water until it melts. Stir the chocolate until smooth.

3 *Whisk* the egg whites until stiff, then *fold* the almonds, sugar, and egg whites into the chocolate until mixed together.

4 Put teaspoons of the mixture on to the baking sheet. *Bake* for 15 to 20 minutes, then move to a wire rack to cool.

Once the macaroons have cooled, store them in an airtight container to keep them crisp.

77

FLAPJACKS

You will need

Baking tin 28 cm by 18 cm
(11 in by 7½ in) • Large saucepan
Wooden spoon • Spoon • Knife • Bowl
Saucepan • Wire rack

For plain flapjacks

Butter for greasing baking tin

 225 g (8 oz) butter

85 g (3 oz) caster sugar

2 tablespoons maple
syrup or honey

340 g (12 oz)
porridge oats

¼ teaspoon salt

For chocolate flapjacks

115 g (4 oz)
dark chocolate

For fruit and nut flapjacks

115 g (4 oz) raisins

55 g (2 oz) flaked almonds

Plain flapjacks

1 Set the oven. *Grease* the baking tin. Put the butter, sugar, and maple syrup or honey in a large pan and melt over a low heat.

2 Take the pan off the heat. Add the oats and salt to the butter mixture and mix everything together well.

3 Tip the mixture into the baking tin and press it down firmly. *Bake* for 20 to 30 minutes, until golden brown.

4 Cut the flapjacks into squares and leave them to cool in the tin. Once they have completely cooled take them out of the tin.

Chocolate flapjacks

1 Make plain flapjacks as above. Then break the chocolate into a bowl and stand it over a saucepan of water.

2 Heat the saucepan of water until it *simmers*. Stir the chocolate as it melts until it forms a smooth chocolate sauce.

3 Dip one end of each piece of flapjack into the melted chocolate, then put it on a wire rack until the chocolate sets.

Fruit and nut flapjacks

Raisins, almonds, and oats make fruit and nut flapjacks an energy-filled snack.

Make as for the plain flapjacks, but add the raisins and almonds to the mixture at the same time as the oats and salt.

An oaty treat

Cook your flapjacks so they are ready when you want them. If you make them early in the afternoon, they will be ready to eat by teatime.

Chocolate flapjack

Plain flapjack

Fruit and nut flapjack

STAINED-GLASS COOKIES

You will need

Baking sheet • Baking parchment
Mixing bowl • Wooden spoon
Sieve • Rolling pin • Biscuit cutters
Sharp knife • Wire rack

Ingredients

	115 g (4 oz) softened butter
	55 g (2 oz) caster sugar
	175 g (6 oz) plain flour
	1-2 tablespoons milk
	Fruit-flavoured boiled sweets

What to do

1 Set the oven. Line a baking sheet with baking parchment. *Beat* the butter and sugar until thick, pale, and creamy.

2 *Sift* in the flour, then mix it into the butter and sugar. Stir in the milk, then knead to form a soft ball of dough.

The cookie holds the sweet in shape.

3 *Roll out* the dough on a floured surface until about ½ cm (¼ in) thick, then cut it into shapes with biscuit cutters.

4 Cut a hole in the middle of each shape and put half a sweet in it. Bake the cookies for about 15 minutes until golden.

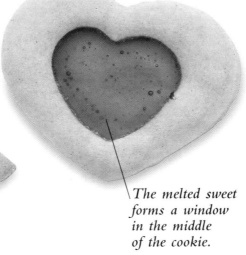

The melted sweet forms a window in the middle of the cookie.

5 Take the cookies out of the oven. When the melted sweets have hardened, move the cookies to a wire rack to finish cooling.

CHOCOLATE DIPS

You will need

Baking sheet • Baking parchment
Mixing bowl • Wooden spoon
Piping bag with medium-sized
star nozzle • Wire rack
Small bowl • Saucepan

Ingredients

 225 g (8 oz) softened butter

55 g (2 oz) icing sugar

 175 g (6 oz) plain flour

55 g (2 oz) cornflour

Few drops vanilla essence

Grated zest of 1 orange

175 g (6 oz) plain
chocolate

Handy hints

If you haven't got a piping bag,
place widely spaced teaspoons
of the biscuit mixture on the
baking sheet instead.

What to do

1 Set the oven and line a
baking sheet with baking
parchment. *Cream* the butter and
sugar together in a mixing bowl.

2 Add the flour, cornflour,
vanilla essence, and orange
zest to the butter mixture and
beat well with a wooden spoon.

3 Put the mixture in a piping
bag and pipe it on to the
baking sheet in short lines. *Bake*
for 15 minutes, until pale golden.

4 Cool the biscuits on a wire
rack. Break the chocolate
into a small bowl and melt it
over a pan of *simmering* water.

5 Dip one end of each biscuit
into the melted chocolate
and lay it on the wire rack until
the chocolate has set.

RASPBERRY MUFFINS

You will need

*Paper cake cases • Muffin tin
Saucepan • Sieve • Bowl
Mixing bowl • Whisk or fork
Wooden spoon • Large metal spoon
Spoon • Wire rack*

Ingredients

115 g (4 oz) butter

285 g (10 oz)
plain flour

1 level tablespoon baking powder

Pinch of salt

2 eggs

85 g (3 oz)
caster sugar

220 ml (8 fl oz) milk

225 g (8 oz) raspberries

85 g (3 oz) white
chocolate drops

Tasty tips

You can make all sorts of muffins.

• Try using 225 g (8 oz)
blackberries, blueberries, or
chopped apricots instead of
the raspberries.

• Instead of white chocolate, try
dark chocolate or chopped nuts.

• To make apple muffins just
add 2 chopped apples and
1 teaspoon ground cinnamon
to the basic recipe.

What to do

1 Set the oven. Put cake cases
in a muffin tin. Melt the
butter in a pan. *Sift* the flour, salt,
and baking powder into a bowl.

2 *Beat* the eggs in a bowl,
then add the sugar, milk,
and melted butter. Add the
flour mixture and *fold* it in.

3 *Fold* the raspberries and
chocolate drops into the
muffin mixture, then spoon it
into the cake cases.

4 *Bake* the muffins for 25 to
30 minutes, until they have
risen and are firm and brown.
Put them on a wire rack to cool.

*The finished
muffins are
light and puffy.*

*Muffins are best
eaten the day
you make them.*

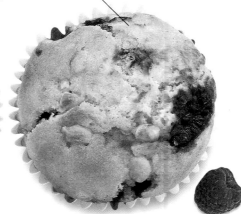

PECAN PUFFS

You will need

2 baking sheets • Mixing bowl
Wooden spoon • Coffee grinder, food
processor, or chopping board and
sharp knife • Sieve • Small sieve
or tea-strainer • Wire rack

Ingredients

Butter for greasing baking sheets

 115 g (4 oz) softened butter

2 tablespoons caster sugar

 140 g (5 oz) pecan nuts
or walnuts

140 g (5 oz) plain flour

A few drops vanilla extract

Icing sugar for dusting

What to do

1 Set the oven and *grease* the baking sheets. *Beat* the butter in a bowl until soft, then *beat* in the sugar until creamy.

2 Chop the nuts very finely or grind them in a coffee grinder or food processor until they are like fine breadcrumbs.

3 Stir the nuts into the butter and sugar, *sift* in the flour, then add the vanilla extract. Mix everything into a soft dough.

4 Roll the dough into balls about the size of walnuts and put them on the baking sheets. *Bake* them for about 35 minutes.

Sift more icing sugar over the pecan puffs once they have cooled.

5 *Sift* icing sugar over the puffs and put them back in the oven for 2 minutes. Then put them on a wire rack to cool.

TASTY TARTS

You will need

Sieve • Mixing bowl • Knife • Spoon Clingfilm • Rolling pin • Biscuit cutters • Bun tin or tart tins • Wire rack • Greaseproof paper • Baking tray • Dried beans • Chopping board Sharp knife • Bowl • Whisk

For the pastry

225 g (8 oz) plain flour

Pinch of salt

115 g (4 oz) butter

1 dessertspoon caster sugar

1 beaten egg yolk

1-2 tablespoons cold water

For the jam tarts

Strawberry jam

Apricot jam

For the fruit tarts

A variety of soft fruit

150 ml (¼ pint) double cream

1 dessertspoon icing sugar

Handy hints

• To make it easier to line the tart tins, scrunch up the greaseproof paper first, then open it out again.

• To make the tarts really quickly, use ready-made shortcrust pastry.

Making the pastry

1 *Sift* the flour and salt into the mixing bowl. Cut the butter into small pieces, then *rub* it into the flour with your fingertips.

2 When the mixture looks like breadcrumbs, add the sugar and beaten egg. Mix in enough water to make a soft ball of dough.

3 Wrap the ball of dough in clingfilm and put it in the fridge for 30 minutes. This will make it easier to *roll out*.

4 Set the oven. *Roll out* the pastry on a floured surface, then use a biscuit cutter to cut out round shapes for the tarts.

Making the jam tarts

1 Lay the rounds of pastry in a bun tin and press them gently into place. Spoon apricot and strawberry jam into them.

2 Decorate the tarts with pastry shapes. *Bake* for about 15 minutes until the pastry is golden brown, then cool on a wire rack.

Making the fruit tarts

1 Line the tart tins with pastry, then line the pastry with greaseproof paper and dried beans. *Bake* for 15 minutes until golden.

2 Leave the pastry cases to cool. Wash and slice the fruit, then whip the cream and icing sugar together in a bowl until stiff.

3 Fill each pastry case with whipped cream, then arrange two or three types of sliced fruit in patterns on top.

Tempting tarts

These tarts make a delicious teatime treat, or you could serve the fruit tarts as a pudding.

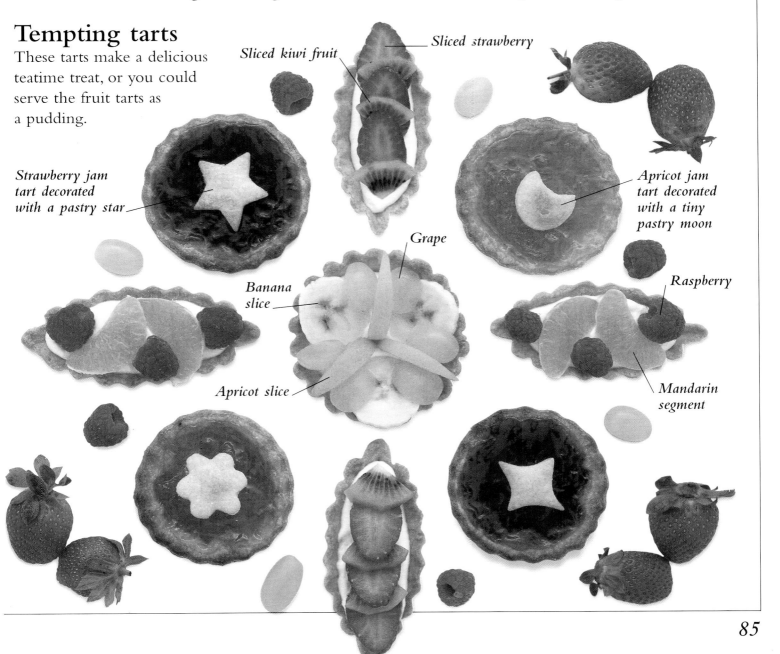

Sliced kiwi fruit

Sliced strawberry

Strawberry jam tart decorated with a pastry star

Apricot jam tart decorated with a tiny pastry moon

Grape

Banana slice

Raspberry

Apricot slice

Mandarin segment

FLORENTINES

You will need

Baking sheet • Baking parchment
Chopping board • Sharp knife
Saucepan • Wooden spoon
Teaspoon • Wire rack • Bowl • Fork

Ingredients

 55 g (2 oz) flaked almonds

55 g (2 oz) glacé cherries

55 g (2 oz) butter

55 g (2 oz) caster sugar

 55 g (2 oz) candied peel

1 tablespoon double cream

115 g (4 oz) dark chocolate

Use a fork to draw wavy lines in the melted chocolate.

What to do

1 Set the oven. Line a baking sheet. Chop the nuts and cherries finely. Melt the butter in a saucepan, then add the sugar.

2 When the sugar dissolves, *boil* the mixture for 1 minute. Take the pan off the heat. Mix in the nuts, cherries, peel, and cream.

3 Put teaspoons of the mixture on to the baking sheet, then *bake* for 10 to 12 minutes until golden brown. Leave to cool.

4 Melt the chocolate in a bowl over a saucepan of *simmering* water. Spread the chocolate on to the backs of the florentines.

CHOCOLATE CRISPY CAKES

You will need

Large bowl • Large saucepan
Wooden spoon • Teaspoon
12 paper cake cases • Baking sheet

Ingredients

225 g (8 oz)
milk chocolate

85 g (3 oz)
cornflakes or
puffed rice

What to do

1 Melt the chocolate in a bowl over a saucepan of *simmering* water. Stir the chocolate from time to time until it is smooth.

2 Add the breakfast cereal to the melted chocolate and stir until the cereal and chocolate are mixed evenly.

The chocolate crispy cakes take about 1 hour to set.

3 Spoon the mixture into the paper cases. Stand them on a baking sheet and leave in a cool place until the chocolate sets.

Store the crispy cakes in an airtight container to keep them fresh.

CHOCOLATE TRUFFLES

You will need

Mixing bowl • Wooden spoon
3 plates or shallow bowls
Paper sweet cases

For the truffles

55 g (2 oz)
cream or curd cheese

55 g (2 oz)
chopped nuts

55 g (2 oz)
icing sugar

30 g (1 oz)
cocoa powder

For the coating

Cocoa powder

Desiccated coconut

Chocolate vermicelli

What to do

1 Put the cream cheese, nuts, icing sugar, and cocoa powder in a bowl and mix together well. Roll the mixture into small balls.

3 Roll the truffles in the cocoa powder, coconut, or vermicelli, to coat them. Put the truffles in paper sweet cases.

2 Put the desiccated coconut, cocoa powder, and chocolate vermicelli on three plates or shallow bowls.

Chocolate truffle coated in cocoa powder

Chocolate truffle coated in desiccated coconut

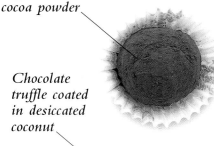

Chocolate truffle coated in chocolate vermicelli

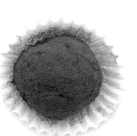

FRUIT AND NUT BALLS

You will need

Baking sheet • Baking parchment
Chopping board and sharp knife, or
food processor • Bowl • Saucepan
Wooden spoon • Paper sweet cases

Ingredients

85 g (3 oz) ready-to-eat
dried apricots

55 g (2 oz)
blanched almonds

55 g (2 oz) raisins

140 g (5 oz)
white chocolate

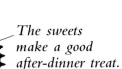

55 g (2 oz)
desiccated coconut

What to do

1 Line a baking sheet with the parchment. Chop the apricots, almonds, and raisins very finely, or whizz them in a food processor.

2 Melt the chocolate in a bowl over a saucepan of *simmering* water. Then stir in the chopped fruit, almonds, and coconut.

3 Roll the mixture into small balls. Put the balls on the baking sheet and leave them to set for 1 to 2 hours.

The sweets make a good after-dinner treat.

When the sweets have set, put them in paper sweet cases.

Keep the sweets in a cool place, so they do not melt.

PEANUT BUTTER SWEETS

You will need

Saucepan • Mixing bowl or food processor • Wooden spoon Baking tray 20 cm (8 in) square Palette knife • Bowl • Sharp knife

For the sweets

55 g (2 oz) butter

55 g (2 oz) dark brown sugar

240 g (8½ oz) smooth peanut butter

200 g (7 oz) icing sugar

For the chocolate topping

175 g (6 oz) dark chocolate or chocolate drops

15 g (½ oz) butter

What to do

1 Melt the butter in a saucepan. Mix it in a bowl with the brown sugar, peanut butter, and icing sugar.

2 Spoon the mixture into the baking tray and spread it out evenly. Press it down firmly on top with a palette knife.

3 Break the chocolate into a bowl and add the butter. Stir them over a saucepan of *simmering* water until they melt.

4 Spread the chocolate over the peanut butter mixture. Leave it to chill until it has set but is still soft enough to cut.

Keep the peanut butter sweets in the fridge until you are ready to eat them.

Peanut butter sweets are good served at a birthday party.

5 Cut the mixture into squares and remove them from the baking tray, then put them in the fridge to finish setting.

PEPPERMINT CREAMS

You will need

Baking sheet • Non-stick baking parchment • Mixing bowl • Whisk Sieve • Wooden spoon • Chopping board Fork • Bowl • Saucepan

Ingredients

 1 egg white

 340 g (12 oz) icing sugar

 A few drops peppermint essence

A few drops each red and green food colouring (optional)

55 g (2 oz) dark chocolate

Tasty tips

Try making orange or lemon creams. Use half a teaspoon of orange or lemon juice instead of the peppermint essence.

What to do

1 Line a baking sheet with baking parchment. Whisk the egg white lightly in a bowl until it is frothy but not stiff.

2 *Sift* the icing sugar into the bowl, then stir it into the egg white with a wooden spoon until the mixture is stiff.

3 Knead in the peppermint essence. Divide the mixture into three balls. Knead food colouring into two of them.

4 Roll the mixture into small balls and put on the baking sheet. Flatten them with a fork, then leave to set for 24 hours.

5 Melt the chocolate in a bowl over a pan of *simmering* water. Dip some of the set peppermint creams into the chocolate.

Chocolate-dipped peppermint cream

Lemon cream with yellow food colouring

Peppermint cream with green food colouring

Peppermint cream with red food colouring

Orange cream with orange food colouring

PICTURE GLOSSARY

This is a picture guide to some of the special terms that cooks often use. Here you can find out what each term means and learn to master the most useful basic cookery skills.

Grilling

To grill food, cook it quickly at a high temperature under a grill. It is best to preheat the grill before cooking the food.

Baking

Baking means cooking food in an oven. Turn on the oven in advance so that it is at the right temperature when you start baking.

Seasoning

To season food, add salt, pepper, spices, or herbs to it. This gives it extra flavour. Taste the food to check if it has enough seasoning.

Frying

Frying means cooking food in a shallow layer of hot fat or oil until it is crisp and golden. Food is usually fried in a frying pan.

Simmering

Simmering means cooking the ingredients over a low heat on top of the cooker so that the liquid is just bubbling.

Marinating

Marinating means soaking food in a sauce called a marinade before cooking. A marinade adds flavour and makes the food more tender.

Stir-frying

To stir-fry food, cook it in a wok or large frying pan with a little oil. Cook it over a high heat and stir it all the time.

Boiling

Boiling means cooking the ingredients over a high heat on top of the cooker so that the liquid bubbles fiercely.

Dicing

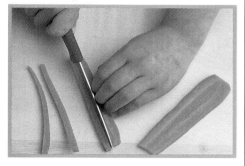

1 Dicing means cutting food into small cubes. To dice a vegetable, cut it in half lengthwise, then cut it into narrow strips.

2 Hold the strips together firmly and slice across them, making small cubes. Move your fingers back carefully as you cut.

Slicing

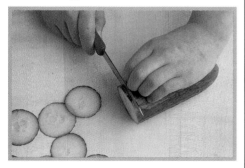

To slice vegetables, hold them firmly on a chopping board and slice downwards. Hold the knife against your knuckles, as shown.

Chopping an onion

1 Peel the papery skin off the onion. Leave the root on as it will help to hold the onion together when you slice it.

2 Cut the onion in half through the root. Lay one half cut-side down and slice downwards using a sharp knife.

3 When you have cut the onion in slices one way, turn the onion and cut across the first slices at right angles.

Shredding a lettuce

Hold the lettuce down on a chopping board and cut across it in fine slices. This will give you thin ribbons of lettuce.

Chopping herbs

To chop fresh herbs, bunch the stalks together and hold them down on a chopping board, then slice across the leaves very finely.

Preparing root ginger

Cut the woody skin off the piece of root. Slice the ginger finely. Cut the slices into thin strips, then cut the strips into small cubes.

Stoning fruit

1 Cut the fruit in half, following the crease down its side. Then twist each half of the fruit to loosen it from the stone.

2 The halves of the fruit will come apart, leaving one half with the stone. Scoop out the stone using a small spoon.

Coring an apple

1 Wash the apple, then hold it on a chopping board. Push the corer into it over the stalk, then push it down to the base.

2 Gently pull the corer out of the apple again. It will contain a cylinder of apple, including the core and the pips.

Beating

To beat something means to stir it hard. Beat eggs with a fork or whisk until the yolks and whites are mixed together completely.

Whisking

To whisk egg whites, beat them lightly and quickly with a whisk or electric mixer until they are firm and stand up in little peaks.

Separating an egg

1 Crack the egg near the middle by tapping it sharply against a bowl. Then break the egg open with your thumbs.

2 Tip the yolk from one half of the shell to the other, so that the white slips into the bowl below. Put the yolk in a separate bowl.

Folding in

This is a gentle way of mixing two things together. Take scoops of the mixture and turn it over and round until it is mixed evenly.

Sifting

To sift flour or icing sugar, shake it through a sieve. This gets rid of any lumps and makes the flour or sugar light and airy.

Rubbing in

Cut the butter into cubes, then rub it into the flour with your fingertips until the mixture looks like breadcrumbs.

Greasing a tin

To grease a baking tin or an ovenproof dish, rub it lightly with butter, oil, or lard. This stops food from sticking to it.

Creaming

1 To cream butter and sugar together, cut up softened butter and mix it with the sugar in a bowl using a wooden spoon.

2 Then beat the butter and sugar together hard until the mixture is pale and creamy and drops off the spoon easily.

Rolling out pastry

1 Sprinkle the table and rolling pin lightly with flour. Flatten the ball of pastry with your hand, then roll it out away from you.

2 Turn the pastry and roll it again, sprinkling it with flour if it sticks. Do this until the pastry is the shape and thickness needed.

Lining a baking tin

1 Lay the cake tin on a piece of greaseproof paper or baking parchment and draw around it. Then cut out the paper shape.

2 Brush the inside of the tin with melted butter. Lay the paper inside. If it is greaseproof paper, brush it with more butter.

INDEX